THE ROADSIDE WILDLIFE BOOK

THE
ROADSIDE
WILDLIFE BOOK

RICHARD MABEY

DAVID & CHARLES

NEWTON ABBOT LONDON
NORTH POMFRET (VT) VANCOUVER

ISBN 0 7153 6781 1

LOC 74–82830

© Richard Mabey 1974

Set in 11 on 13pt Garamond
by Avontype (Bristol) Ltd
and printed in Great Britain
by Redwood Burn Limited, Trowbridge & Esher
for David & Charles (Holdings) Limited
South Devon House Newton Abbot Devon

Published in the United States of America
by David & Charles Inc
North Pomfret Vermont 05053 USA

Published in Canada
by Douglas David & Charles Ltd
3645 McKechnie Drive West Vancouver BC

Contents

Illustrations

8

PART ONE

THE ROAD

Introduction

The first country road I remember was one my father wheeled me along in a push-chair most Sunday mornings during the last years of the war. We used to begin at a small air-raid shelter, and trudge up between a tunnel of overhanging hazel and may. For a quarter of a mile or so out of the town it was an ordinary enough lane, passing the grounds of a foundling school and two scraggy strips of woodland. But if we kept on due south towards the edge of the chalk, instead of turning west for the pub, the landscape suddenly changed. On our left an arable field strewn with poppies and partridges sloped away from the wood. The lane skirted it, then dropped sharply and abruptly to the left, down into the valley of a stream which they used to say flowed only in time of war. The tarmac gave way to rough gravel, the low field-side hedges to steep banks of holly and oak and traveller's joy, and at the bottom of the zig-zag track was an old farmhouse, picked out in rich orange against the dark foliage of the nearby Scots pines. We could have been in the heart of the West Country instead of at the edge of the Home Counties commuter belt.

I suspect that everyone has a lane like this somewhere amongst their childhood memories, if only a cobbled city back-street overlooked by the planners which gave a welcome escape route from the regimented boredom of housing estates. They have a special nostalgic magic, these narrow tracks; an intimacy built on familiarity. I must have been down that Chiltern lane a thousand times since the war. I have seen many of the hedges go down, pylons straddle the now dried-up stream and a motorway creep towards the farmhouse. Yet for me it is still the most enchanting lane in England, and the surprise I feel when that valley opens out round the bend is undiminished.

I think the affection we have for these roads is born in part from the security they offer, not just in the familiar landscapes to which they lead, but in the way their boundaries of hedges and cottages enclose us without suffocating us. In the countryside they are meeting places between the human and the natural worlds, an intimate network of ways through the very fabric of the landscape.

But now children are ferried along such lanes in cars, not push-chairs, and road traffic has become one of our chief environmental villains. Many conservationists indeed would pick out the auto-mobile as the single most damaging product of industrial society. New roads to carry it can raze whole streets to the ground. Farms are cut in half and woods flattened. Energy reserves are burnt up – in totally unproductive traffic jams as likely as not – and spewed out as toxic gases. Beauty spots are choked not only by these fumes but by more metal and human visitors than they can ever cope with. Looking at the way our landscape is changing, it's difficult not to become cynical about the planners' priorities: cars come first, houses, food and peaceful living a very poor second.

This might be the conservationist's view of the impact of road transport on our environment. It's a bleak view, and a generalised one, but only someone severely blinkered by vested interests would be likely to contradict it completely.

Ask a motorist for his view of cars and the countryside, and you're likely to get a rather different impression. It's not that he'll deny the damage the car deals out, but it's a price he's prepared to pay, and in any case is not usually part of his *experience* of motoring. For him the car represents a way out of the city, and a chance of exploring those childhood lanes again. Maybe it took his children on their first trip to the sea, and to the commons where they go blackberrying in the autumn. The car for him is an amenity, one way of bringing people and the countryside together.

From an urban point of view cars and the countryside are

inseparable. Towns are where we live and work – 'stay put', in fact. The countryside is for travelling – either through or to. Indeed, how much of the variety of the British landscape would we know if we hadn't glimpsed it through car and train windows? For most people natural history begins not at home but on the road.

So we have two views of the impact of the car: the destroyer and the liberator. Both are true and both describe parts of the complex relationship between the traveller and the countryside. In this book I've concentrated on those aspects of this relationship that concern the natural world. What has travelling man done to wayside wildlife, and what enjoyment can he get from it?

I said travelling man rather than motorised man as the story of this relationship begins long before the car, and before the road for that matter. It's easy to forget that without tracks of some sort we would know virtually nothing of our countryside. We'd be able neither to move about nor, you might say, see the wood beyond the trees. A pathway is just as natural a habitat as a nest, the environment of a mobile, land-based animal going about its business. Even our smallest mammals, the shrews, have thready driveways up to their holes.

It was only when paths began to be used so regularly by men that they were deliberately managed to make the going easier, that a quite new sort of habitat was created. The road is a unique environment, a strip of ground cleared to varying extents of vegetation and enclosed by complex borders of grassland, bushes, water and non-living gadgets. None of these of course is exclusive to roads and you'll find bits of them on any patch of scrubland or meadow. But remember how closely and intimately they're meshed here; that there are something like 150,000 miles of metalled road in Britain, most of it edged in this way; that moving past this wallpapering of greenery is the closest many of us get to the wildlife of our countryside, and you see what a crucial role roads can play in conserving wildlife and encouraging its appreciation. Cars themselves are another matter, as we'll see, but without roads and tracks much of our countryside would be a uniform, impenetrable, inscrutable and unvarying forest.

I imagine there will be some readers who will not be convinced that a road is a sufficiently 'pure' habitat (like an oak wood, say) to justify writing a general book about its natural life. What, they might reasonably ask, has the wildlife of a gutter to do with that of the nearby hedge? Isn't the connection really nothing more than a physical coincidence, of no ecological significance whatsoever? What is there in common between the verge flowers of a Roman road through the Fens, a Devon lane, a motorway across the Pennines? And what conceivable association can there be between the secretive birds of a Scottish mountain pass and those touting for titbits in a suburban layby?

It's undeniably true that roads are complex habitats, that their location and underlying soil and the type of farming practised nearby all have a deep influence on their natural life. But all roads do have one species in common: travelling man, usually inside the disposable metal shell he uses for migration. It is this creature that any study of roadside natural history must be chiefly concerned with, and the way his behaviour influences the creatures he shares this environment with. The wildlife of that Pennine motorway is indeed different from that of a narrow lane in the Shires. But the fact that they are both used by man as pathways imposes a pattern, a style, on the way these species live, feed, travel and die.

This pattern is the theme of this book. Since the road is (after the garden) the semi-natural landscape with which man is likely to be most intimate, there's no better place for coming to grips, first-hand, with some of the basics of ecology. For it is *you*, in your car, and all those organisations you pay to make your journey quicker and safer, that are the chief influences on the surrounding wildlife – not, as is usually the case, some remote international mining company or factory farmer.

If all this sounds heavy and off-putting, and a far cry from those childhood expeditions after frogspawn and wayside glow-worms, let me say that I've tried to include as much as I can on casual encounters with wildlife on the road, as on the more massive changes brought about by the construction of a new motorway, say. Most of us have met a toad on the road, or wondered what on earth a kestrel could be looking for hovering over a six-lane motorway. Human pathways inevitably cross animal territories and tracks, and these encounters are part of the fun of travelling.

And I've tried to treat the motorist as fairly as possible. He built many of the roads, after all, and arguably has as much right as any other predator to lord it over his territory. There are even occasions, as we shall see, when new roads can actually benefit certain species.

But no predator is a vandal to quite the extent that motorised man is, and much of the second half of this book takes a fairly stern look at the indiscriminate and gratuitous destruction which the motorcar is dealing out in its own habitat. The first part is chiefly concerned with the structure of the road as a habitat, regardless of how it is being used.

One huge subject that I have only touched on, even though it underpins all the others, is the *social* impact of motor traffic in the countryside. This is a natural history book, after all, and I did not feel it was the place to discuss problems of traffic congestion, road-routing, parking etc, except in so far as they affect wildlife.

Uninhibited walkers in the Goyt Valley in the Peak District after the experimental scheme to ban traffic from this beauty spot (see page 150)

For fascinating and thorough discussions of these essentially planning problems, I recommend particularly chapter 15 of Nan Fairbrother's *New Lives, New Landscapes* and J. Allan Patmore's *Land and Leisure* (see the bibliography for more details of these books and some of the more local studies of the impact of the car on the countryside).

Nevertheless, I couldn't ignore these issues altogether, for the way cars are managed in the countryside ultimately determines their effect on the natural world just as much as on the human world. So in my conclusion I've looked at some of the schemes which are being used, experimented with, or just dreamed about, for making the car less of a menace in our countryside. In the end the sufferings of a crew-cut wayside hedge and a jammed-up weekend tourist have the same cause, and will likely have the same solution.

A broadside pedlar

A short history of the road

There were trackways through the countryside long before there were human travellers. Most mammals use regular paths between their sleeping and breeding sites and the places they go to feed and drink. If you've ever explored the area around a badger sett you will know how easy it is to trace the routes of their nightly meanderings from the tunnels through the undergrowth and the worn earth.

Early man no doubt cashed in on these ready-made paths (he would often, after all, be chasing the same water supply and occasionally the animals themselves) and other naturally levelled routes, like dried-up river beds. But with the coming of stone and iron tools the forest could be cleared and more ambitious paths cut. Many of these prehistoric trackways kept, for safety's sake, to high ground, and there are still relics of 'ridgeways' in parts of our countryside.

It was with the settled communities of the Celts – and later the Saxons – that we find the beginning of roads as we know them now, and of that familiar pattern of edging that has made roads so crucial for wildlife.

The social and administrative system at this time meant that tracks were regulated not only by the lie of the land but by the complex details of land tenure. If the boundary between two settlements or estates was a serpentine one, then the track between them would be too. It's possible that some of the sunken lanes in Devon, and those curious 'green lanes' apparently going nowhere, still follow the paths of ditches cut out to mark the boundaries between the two farms. The excavated soil was piled up in banks several feet high on either side of the ditch, creating the first artificial wayside habitats.

This respect for land boundaries survived right up until the Parliamentary Enclosures, and accounts for many of those inexplicable doublings-back and dog-leg bends in our country lanes. There's a delightful if rather less credible explanation from East Anglia, where it's said that the local roadbuilders would only work with their backs to the immutable winds of that region. When these veered, the workmen tacked with them!

The Romans, being an occupying power, weren't bothered by their subjects' territorial arrangements. Their roads were functional trade and military routes, and were cut along the shortest practical paths between the points they serviced. Hence their legendary straightness. Yet these roads had a number of features that we associate with modern country lanes and highways, and had a significant effect upon our flora. As far as can be judged from contemporary descriptions, most of the Roman roads in this country were built on embankments, or 'aggers'. Sometimes these were as much as four or five feet above the surrounding countryside. Daniel Defoe, writing in the 1720s, describes the Fosse Way as still being raised eight or nine feet in many places.

Between AD 40 and 80, the Romans laid something like 6,500 miles of highway. (Were these raised roads one origin of this word?) Like the embankments and cuttings of modern motorways, the artificial slopes of these 'aggers' provided something like 6,000 acres of grassland, ripe for colonisation not only by native field flowers, but by foreign weeds. Stretching as they did between Exeter and Richborough in the south and the Antonine wall in Scotland, they provided a countrywide distribution system for these plants.

Since much of the earth for these embankments must have been dug out of ditches on either side, the complete road complex provided a wide range of habitats. There would be a graduated range of drainage and moisture from the occasionally paved surface of the road itself down to the damp ditch-bottom. The sunny south-facing slopes must have been especially congenial for colonisation by the southern European plants brought over by the settlers;

moving continually along these roads were 40,000 Roman troops and the traffic carrying their imported food crops and cattle fodder. Native weeds from the Mediterranean would inevitably be caught up in these, and their seeds spilled onto the embankments, from whence many of them spread into the adjoining arable land.

It's impossible to say for certain which of our wayside and cornfield flowers were introduced accidentally in this way, but evidence of the following plants – all weeds, in the sense that they are only found where humans are disturbing the ground – only begins to appear in deposits dating back to the Roman period: corn cockle, scarlet pimpernel, greater celandine, Scotch thistle, white mustard, sowthistle, field woundwort. Others, like fennel, ground elder (goutweed) and henbane, may have been introduced deliberately as medicinal herbs. Roadsides are still amongst their favourite habitats (see pp. 68 and 150).

Away from the main Roman roads, the appallingly muddy condition of most of the lanes must have been even more favourable to the distribution of plant seeds. (Look at what that ballad vendor was traipsing through on page 18.) The roads got steadily worse as more and more heavy carriages began to use them. Defoe called one of the main northbound roads near Dunstable 'perfectly frightful for travellers'. Those responsible for the upkeep of the roads campaigned vigorously against wheeled traffic using their paths at all, complaining with some justification that wheels played havoc with the soft road surface, and that if they were to be allowed, they ought to be wide enough to act as rollers.

It was this chaotic and deteriorating situation that gave birth to the Turnpike Trusts – random groups of local people, who in return for offering to build and maintain a section of highway were given the right in 1663 to put up gates and charge a toll on all travellers. A few did their job properly, but most carried on, as Clough Williams-Ellis has said, 'more as a private racket than a public service'. They levied just about every living creature and inanimate vehicle that passed along their roads, but ignored their contractual obligations to build and maintain. It was not until 1832, when Parliament handed over responsibility for road upkeep

to the newly-fashioned parish authorities, that things began to improve.

The great development in cattle and particularly sheep trade from the sixteenth century onwards meant that there were vast numbers of animals moving about the countryside between the farms and the great fairs and markets. They tended to keep to the traditional drove roads and trackways. The new roads – particularly those of the Turnpike Trusts – would not only have entangled them with heavy traffic but also with grasping tollkeepers. And even if a flock could rest for a while without being run down by a coach-and-four, there would not be much for them to graze on in the churned-up mire. But along the quieter and more gently worn drove roads there were wide verges of fine turf, grazed by generations of migrating cattle. There was fodder for their human companions too: many old inns which appear to be stuck irrationally off any major route were established to quench the thirst of those dusty drovers.

With the coming of the railways the drove roads fell into disuse, but some have now formed the routes for modern surfaced roads,

A section of the Roman Road at Blackstone Edge in Yorkshire, which ran towards Ilkley over the very top of the Pennines. This is the most remarkable surviving stretch of Roman road in Britain, showing very clearly the vestigial verges, drainage ditches, and the stone cobbles with which the more important roads were faced. The combination of those boot-scraping stones and the typical Roman military sandal with its multitude of hobnails, must have been ideal for transferring seed-carrying mud down onto the road, making these roads a real force in distributing plants around our countryside.

The botanist H. T. Clifford, experimenting with mud scraped from modern footwear, succeeded in raising 43 different species of plant from a representative sample of shoes. And Sir Edward Salisbury, never at a loss for a delightfully eccentric experiment, achieved similar results with the dust swept from under church pews. The churches were selected on the basis of having long paved or cobbled approaches, so that the mud from which the dust was derived would have been transported for at least that distance.

23

Hampshire Down sheep and shepherd on a drove road near Stonehenge, 1901

and a few are left in their original condition. Along these tracks – and indeed along many dry grassy roadsides – you will find flowers whose names testify to the crucial role sheep played in shaping the flora of our grasslands. Sheep's gowan (white clover) and sheep's fescue grass were gorged by the animals. Sheepsbit, sheep's bells (harebells in Dorset) and sheep's knapperty (tormentil) flourished in the fine sward produced by their grazing. The shepherds, too, laid an affectionate claim to some of the flowers that were their companions on the lonely drove roads and pastures. Milkwort became shepherd's thyme on the Wiltshire downs; squinancywort (not such an odd name as it sounds: it was taken for the quinsy) was a Somerset shepherd's bedstraw; and on the Northumberland fells the yellow-flowered mountain pansy that is one of the ancestors of our modern garden pansies pleased the herdsmen enough for them to name it as their own.

Unlike their charges, shepherds had nothing much to nibble in the grass. But at least they had a barometer, of sorts, in the scarlet pimpernel. All through sheep country you will find local names which acknowledge this plant's habit of closing its red blooms in gloom or damp or with a drop in temperature. It is shepherd's clock in Gloucestershire, shepherd's glass in Norfolk, shepherd's warning in Lincolnshire, and shepherd's weatherglass in half a dozen counties from Devon to Yorkshire.

But meanwhile some efforts were being made to maintain a navigable road system. These were the days of the Parliamentary Enclosures, and a great number of country roads were built to service the new field configurations. Most were as geometrically ordered as the enclosed fields themselves. They ran straight across country, as logically – and insensitively – as any Roman highway. Old feudal boundaries were ignored, isolated farmhouses and whole hamlets left stranded, or at best reached by small sideroads.

But they were good and serviceable roads for all their lack of character. To avoid the miserable conditions which still existed on the earlier generation of highways, the Enclosure legislation normally specified a minimum width for a road. An award made in 1748 in Warwickshire ordered that the road between Burton-upon-Trent and Atherstone should not be less than 100 feet wide. This is an immense size for an eighteenth century road (it's about the same as a three-lane motorway) and reflects just how much unsurfaced roads tended to expand as drivers made detours past the most rutted or boggy patches. The main London to Exeter road was said to have been over a quarter of a mile across by the end of an average winter, where it ploughed through the soft chalk on Salisbury Plain.

This policy of minimum road widths was responsible for the creation of the verge as we know it today. At the close of the eighteenth century it had become a fairly general rule that an inter-village enclosure road should be about forty feet wide, ditched on both sides, and paved with stones down the middle wherever possible, to a width of between twelve and fifteen feet. This left grass verges about twelve feet wide on either side of the central carriageway – quite broad enough for a coach to make a detour should the centre of the road become impassable in winter. And behind these, the rows of field oaks and newly planted hawthorns, set down to stop these diversions meandering into the neighbouring fields.

We are still a hundred years away from the first motor vehicles, and only just into the age when Telford and Macadam began applying engineering principles to road surfacing. Yet already the pattern of the roadside habitat as we know it had been set: a central carriageway bordered by a grass verge, a ditch and a hedge.

It is a pattern which has remained essentially unaltered for two centuries. Even the dimensions are much the same. Over much of farming England most straight country roads still measure a dozen paces from hedge to hedge.

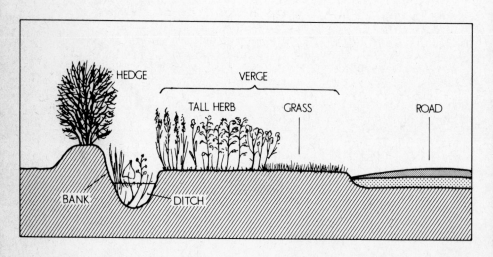

The main elements of the road as a natural habitat: the road surface, often cambered so that seeds and leaves are washed into the gutter; the grass verge itself, often supporting at least two different types of plant community, according to the way it is mown; the drainage ditch, containing aquatic vegetation, and often sloping up towards the hedge to form a sunny bank; the hedge itself.

The road surface

The actual surface of the road seems the least promising of all wayside habitats. By definition, it's a strip cleared of vegetation and in all probability sealed over with tarmac. But if it's got few natural residents as a result, it's not short on human activity. It is the by-products of this that make the road itself a veritable supermarket for birds shopping around for an easy meal. Think of the odd titbits that find their way out of your car window and you'll see the range of food that's available to gregarious scroungers like sparrows. But it's grain and seed above all that attracts the birds: winnowed off roadside grasses, ferried by tyres, spilled off the backs of grain lorries and farm wagons.

There are some birds which seem to have a special liking for tarmac feeding. Adaptable scavengers like sparrows and starlings are to be expected. But why does one so often flush pied wagtails – very deft jaywalkers, by the way – from the carriageway? Are they feeding on insects killed by traffic? Or do they see the burnished surface of a metalled road as something close to the streamside rocks and shallow pools that are their favourite feeding grounds? It's not unknown for an exhausted sea duck, blown inland by winter gales, to crash-land on a wet road surface after mistaking it for open water.

You may startle a pair of turtle doves on roads through open land at harvest time. They may be after scattered corn or fumitory seeds, which they will devour in preference to all other grain. But they would find these more easily at the field edge, and I suspect they may be sunning themselves on the warm tarmac.

Sadly, as we shall see, the motorcar doesn't just flush birds from

It's not just food scraps that the road surface provides. These house martins are collecting mud for nest-building from an unmetalled road.

Not gutter snipes, but house sparrows, taking advantage of some spilled grain

the road. It also turns them into meals for carrion feeders like crows and gulls. In areas where there is a high rabbit population – and consequently many vulnerable young rabbits at certain seasons – I have seen gulls patrolling the road edges apparently waiting for them to be knocked down.

Worms are also commonly seen on carriageways and pavements, and it's something of a mystery why such numbers should be seen on these apparently sterile surfaces. In fact very few roads and pavements are lacking a few cracks, and it's through these that worms rise to the surface at night and after rain. But it's a sight more difficult for them to find their way back again, and the fate of most roadbound worms is to be run over or picked off by blackbirds. Yet the supply of worms under sealed-off surfaces like roads seems to be as inexhaustible as under open soil. During the excavation of some buildings dating from the fourth century at St Albans, large numbers of thriving mudworms were found. This particular population had probably been buried without access to fresh air for fifteen hundred years, yet had managed to find sufficient food to survive.

I was originally going to photograph this endearing fungus, which grew for two autumns out of the gutter in a busy Hertfordshire town centre. But the Highways Department got there before me and rebuilt the kerb as part of a road-widening scheme. We may yet see it again though. For this toadstool was coprinus atramentarius (*close relative of the inky caps, page 108*) *notorious miner of tennis courts and cracker of concrete.*

It's difficult to believe that any toadstool, however sturdy, could exert sufficient pressure to break open a road surface, but they do. One specimen of *Coprinus atramentarius* was noted 'still bearing, like a mortar-board, the piece of asphalt that it had broken and pushed up'. This was nothing, though, compared to the herculean inky cap in Basingstoke which, in 1820, raised a 30 × 24 inch paving stone $1\frac{1}{2}$ inches above the surrounding pavement in 48 hours.

Under the stone 'near the centre was a very large mushroom about the size of a tea-saucer, much flattened at the top'.

Apparently this street had been troubled by fungi before, to such an extent that paving stones 'were upturned, and on taking them up mushrooms were found to be the cause, so troublesome did it become that part of the mould was removed and fresh substituted to get rid of the spawn'.

One last curiosity about *c. atramentarius*. Like its better-known cousin it is perfectly edible – provided no alcohol is drunk with the meal which includes it. In this combination it has a strange effect on the taker: a short time afterwards he begins to feel sick and his face, and occasionally his neck and arms, turn purple. The same effect is produced by the drug antabuse, used in the treatment of alcoholism, and it's believed that the active ingredients may be related.

The grass verge

The grass verge fulfils much the same role today as it did in the eighteenth and nineteenth centuries. It's still a strip of reserve land, useful for giving roads room to spread, and for forming a barrier between the traveller's territory and the farmer's. No man's land, in a sense – only these days one of the verge's functions is to carry human walkers on its surface, and their domestic services underneath. Other functions of the modern verge are to ensure safe visibility round bends; provide a place to pull vehicles off the road in case of emergency, and a site for salt, gravel and other road maintenance materials; and to give structural support to the road foundations. In fact verges are ruled resolutely by human activity, and by the traffic that passes over and alongside them.

Yet the notion of a grassy verge still conjures up an image which is unequivocally natural and pastoral. Indeed, 'wayside' is almost a synonym for 'wild' when we are talking about flowers. The country lanes with their borders of celandine, primrose, violet, cow parsley and buttercup are one of the great threads of continuity in our countryside, spanning not just our whole island, but centuries of history, too. Edward Thomas, in his poem *Lob*, talks of his hero, a kind of mythical yeoman of England

> Calling the wild cherry tree the merry tree,
> The rose campion Bridget-in-her-bravery;
> And in a tender mood he, as I guess,
> Christened one flower Love-in-idleness,
> And while he walked from Exeter to Leeds
> One April called all cuckoo flowers Milkmaids.

From him old herbal Gerard learnt, as a boy,
To name wild clematis the Traveller's joy.
from Collected Poems (1936)

In these narrow strips of grass, comparatively safe from the plough, the historical continuity can be quite literal. You can still find the scarce bastard balm, a startlingly vivid member of the mint family, in the lanes of the limestone country around Totnes where it was first recorded in the 1650s.

Though they have often had a hard fight against ruthless mowing and weedkilling programmes, most of our favourite common wildflowers bloom here too. And with the bluebells, wild straw-berries and celandines there will be cowslips, vetches and poppies, driven out of the fields by modern agricultural techniques, just as

Cow parsley in Redgrave, Suffolk. A delightful and abundant verge blossom, and probably the most important landscape flower in our countryside. How much less attractive this old wall and barn would look without this frothy and exuberant border. The only thing that spoils the view is that stiff and emaciated ornamental cherry, looking as awkwardly out of place as a chrysanthemum would on a Welsh hilltop.

effectively as the public have been excluded by the prairie field system and the loss of thousands of miles of hedgeside footpaths. Road verges are one of the few sectors of ordinary countryside to which the townsman has legal access. It's fortunate that wild flowers should have been able to find refuge there as well, to brighten up the edges of laybys and pavements.

The strictly biological and ecological significance of roadside verges is scarcely less important than their amenity value. There are estimated to be nearly 500,000 acres of verge (including ditches, etc) in the British Isles, an area of land that exceeds that allocated for statutory Nature Reserves. Over 600 of our 2,000 species of flowering plant have been recorded on them, and together with their adjoining hedges they're lived on by 20 species of mammal, 40 birds, 6 reptiles, 25 butterflies and 6 bumble bees.

In many areas they represent the last relics of the semi-natural grassland that under an earlier style of husbandry was abundant in our countryside. But it is the variety that they add to the living landscape that makes verges so biologically rich and exciting. It's a rare verge that is nothing more than a flat plain of grass. Most have short turf, tall herbage and rough scrub, in addition to the ditches and hedges which we'll be considering separately. If a road has been cut through a wood, a whole range of light-loving species will be added to the woodland flora: buttercups, stitchworts, bedstraws, and campions. And as a bonus for the traveller, woodland species which are tolerant of light like bluebells, wood anemones and primroses, will come out of the shade and spill out over the verge.

Road verges can be hosts for rare plants as much as for our common 'wayside' species. At least 27 out of the 300 rarest British plant species occur on road verges. In addition to the perennial flax, there are 6 species for which roadsides are the chief habitat: field cow-wheat, grape hyacinth, clove-scented broomrape, spiked rampion, Plymouth pear, and *beta trigyna*. One species, the sickle hare's-ear, a beautiful yellow-flowered member of the carrot family, had its only known site on a verge near Ongar in Essex. Unfortunately it became extinct there after roadworks in 1955. In

34

Cambridge the only remaining site for the Spanish catchfly is a bank on a roadside near Chippenham. Most of the other sandy areas where it used to grow have been destroyed by ploughing. That exquisitely beautiful orchid the violet helleborine somehow manages to flower occasionally on a roadside in Hampshire.

There are any number of factors which influence the flora of the verge. Firstly, the underlying soil, which is always a limiting feature. The flora of a rough clay verge will never match that of a chalk bank.

Secondly, there are factors like incline, drainage and aspect. The flora of a south-facing banked verge will be different from that on the opposite side of the road because of the greater intensity of sunlight it receives. A north-facing bank is always damper and cooler and will likely be richer in mosses and liverworts.

History inevitably plays a role too. We have seen already how the Romans unwittingly introduced a whole range of Mediterranean weeds along the edges of their roads. Most of these have now spread across the country, and no individual specimen found growing by a Roman road could really have its origins confidently attributed to a centurion's sandal. But along with these introduced species there were other grassland species (like the Watling Street thistle, *eryngium campestre*) which migrated naturally back into Britain as the ice retreated 10,000 years ago. The landscape then was an open, treeless waste in which they were able to flourish. But as the climate improved and forest began to cover the countryside and blanket them out, they were forced into pockets of ground like river banks and cliff faces, where trees couldn't become established.

There they were confined until early man's roadmaking activities began to recreate, artificially, their natural habitats. Our ancient trackways (where they haven't been disturbed) can act as museums for these species, many of which are on the edge of their range in this country. The scarce perennial flax, a species more happy in central Europe, is rare except along the edges of these old roads, particularly the Icknield Way and the Via Devena. It wasn't introduced by the Romans, but the long historical stability of the verges along Roman roads has helped it to survive.

History enters in another way, because where there are roads there are houses and gardens. One of the delights of our village lanes is the way that cottage flowers like honesty, dame's violet and pink oxalis spill out from the gardens and creep along the hedgebanks. The movement is often the other way, too, as with the wild sea pinks that colonise garden walls along the clifftops in Wales and the West Country.

Where a village is very old you will sometimes find survivors from herbal and physic gardens. They may live on long after the cottages in which they were cultivated have vanished. Plants like elecampane, our nearest wild equivalent of the sunflower; alexanders, introduced by the Romans and cultivated as a pot-herb and gout remedy up to the eighteenth century; clary ('clear-eye'), a relative of the garden sage, whose seeds were soaked in water until they swelled up like frogspawn and were then used as a salve for sore eyes; and, perhaps most fascinating of all, lilac-flowered vervain.

Vervain was described as 'comely by way and gate' as early as the end of the fourteenth century. It has a history of use in folk-medicine and magic that goes back to the Druids, when offerings of honey were poured onto the earth from which it was dug. The plant was picked with the left hand, during the rising of the Dog Star when neither sun nor moon were shining.

Just why vervain should have been regarded as so sacred in Saxon lore is not easy to see, but belief in its powers persisted up to the sixteenth century. It was used not just against witchcraft but against many of the most devastating diseases of the time, particularly scrofula, 'the King's Evil'. The faith in it was so strong – understandably, for what other remedies could sufferers turn to then – that its magical and pagan associations were readily accepted by Christianity. John White, in his book *The Way of the True Church* (1608), records this charm which was recited as the herb was picked:

Hallowed be thou, Vervein, as thou growest on the ground,
For in the mount of Calvary there thou was first found.

Autumn crocuses naturalised along the A41 outside Berkhamsted in Hertfordshire. Road verges can be hosts for rare plants as much as for our common 'wayside' species.

37

Thou healest our Saviour Jesus Christ, and stanchedst
　his bleeding wound;
In the name of the Father, the Son and the holy Ghost,
　I take thee from the ground.

The verge flora is also influenced by the agricultural use of the land on the other side of the hedge. Melilot, common as an impurity in certain crops and grass-seed mixtures and sometimes deliberately sown for fodder, is becoming increasingly common on newly-made verges adjacent to arable land.

A group of school children working on a study of the M4 in Wiltshire (see Bibliography) found that along a stretch of nearby road, clovers in all cases started as a large patch near the field entrances and then spread in a clearly-marked line towards the pavement. One of the children, Michael Atwell, aged 13, remarked: 'Animals and man would move in this direction from each field to the farm along the road. Here was clear evidence of the distribution of this plant by animal and man.'

But it is the deliberate human management of the verges that is the most important influence on their plant life, and before beginning to regret this as yet another unhappy instance of human interference, we should remember that without management of some sort, grass verges would vanish. In less than ten years they would simply be extensions of the hedge.

Although the precise ownership of grass verges is shrouded by legal technicalities – boundary hedges and ditches are usually the property of those who own the land adjacent to the road – it is nearly always the responsibility of the local Highways Department to maintain them.

The first and overriding purpose of management, as seen by the county authorities, is to ensure the safety of road users. This means guaranteeing good visibility at bends, cutting back overhanging plants, and providing good drainage of the road surface. But there are many other aims. Pedestrians have to be given room to move, farmland must be protected from invasion by weeds established on the verges and there must be a degree of access (for maintenance workers) to the hedges and ditches at the boundary of the verge.

There will need to be passing places on narrow roads, a sufficient area to accommodate cleared snow during the winter and last – and by no means least, even in the Highways Departments' eyes – there are all those aims included under the term 'amenity'. These include an attempt to give the whole road area a pleasant appearance, to blend it as far as possible into the surrounding countryside, and to consider the recreational needs of walkers, picknickers, naturalists etc.

The problem, of course, is that it's not easy to satisfy all these aims at once. The conflict between them is what has made the management of verges such a controversial issue over recent years. One extreme, but by no means uncommon, view was expressed in the following editorial in an East Anglian newspaper.

As travellers between Ipswich and Hadleigh will have noticed, West Suffolk County Council is carrying out a road improvement plan from Lady Lane to Wolves Wood.*

Although the first inch of new road has yet to be laid, a remarkable improvement has already been made, by the elimination of the hedgerows and roadside flora. The motorist now has a clear view across the many bends, on which heavy lorries used to be able to hold up the traffic for long periods.

People with ample leisure will no doubt regret the loss of plant life; but this is preserved to rather better advantage in the county's country parks. To most drivers, cow-parsley, thistles and nettles and the like are not only unattractive in themselves; but towering above the banks, they add considerably to the difficulties of negotiating winding roads.

The stretch of the A1071 from Wolves Wood offers a good illustration of this. East Suffolk is less concerned about the route to Hadleigh than West, and is in no hurry to improve this stretch of road.

Here, the grass is cut back on the verges, presumably for the benefit of the pedestrians. More violent pruning, particu-

*Wolves Wood itself is now a Royal Society for the Protection of Birds reserve.

39

larly on the inside of the many bends, would do something to rectify the council's neglect of the traffic using the road.

'Road with a View', *East Anglian Daily Times* (24 July 1971)

Although this was written as late as 1971, it already seems an outdated, narrow-minded and certainly over-simplified viewpoint. Nettles and thistles aren't the natural flora of road-verges – they're usually the result of disturbance to the ground. Cow parsley is arguably one of the most attractive wayside flowers. The country parks are few and hard to find and often as tidily shorn of wild flowers in their most public areas as any urban recreation ground.

But I think the most disturbing assumption behind this editorial is that when a man becomes 'a motorist' he somehow becomes part of a different species, with special privileges and priorities. Behind the wheel he is no longer concerned with any human needs, nor, it all too often seems, the needs of any other humans – notice those digs at 'pedestrians' and 'people with ample leisure' – beyond those necessary for moving his vehicle effortlessly along its course.

Of course motorists need, and have a right to expect, good visibility on roads they have helped pay for. Of course ragged outcrops of docks would be better replaced, but surely by buttercups rather than by tarmac or razored grass. The leisure motorist is usually a country lover of some sort, otherwise he'd do his Sunday cruising round the city centres. He and his passengers are going to enjoy their outings considerably more if the highways they are travelling on are more wildly and colourfully bordered than suburban roads.

I think that we now recognise that in a small island where accessible countryside is at a premium, roadside verges must fulfil increasingly complex functions. They must help satisfy not only the non-motoring needs of the carbound, but also the needs of all those other creatures who use them, from pedestrians to earthworms.

It's interesting to compare the outlook of that editorial with another statement made in the same year, from the same corner of England. It was part of a directive from the Deputy Divisional

Road Engineer of the Eastern Region to all the County Councils and other road-minding bodies in his area:

> Grass cutting should never be carried out merely to produce a tidy effect. Tidiness is not synonymous with the best interests of amenity, except in urban areas. It has been said that frequent grass mowing is no more expensive than one or two cuts per year. Nevertheless, infrequent cutting is more desirable as it does encourage a varied and interesting flora, whereas regular cutting is a completely negative approach to grass maintenance.

But need there be such a conflict between the demands of road safety and conservation? No one could deny that there have been some bitter battles in the past; and paradoxically, if it hadn't been for the brutal weedkilling and mowing programmes of the sixties we might never have realised just what a treasure we had in our verges. But the increasing public concern about our countryside has made its impact in the Highways Departments' offices, and the situation had undoubtedly improved over recent years. As is nearly always the case, ways can be found of making a reconciliation.

Those responsible for maintaining grass verges have always had to operate inside this framework of conflicting demands, not to say the limitations of their purses. Before formal verges existed, there was no problem. The land at the edge of a road was normally just part of the adjacent farmland, and was kept tidy because cattle were put out to graze on it. This, of course, is still done along many minor roads in upland Britain.

The vast new area of verge created alongside the Enclosure roads saw the advent of the 'lengthsman', a labourer responsible for the maintenance of the verges along a fixed length of highway. These he would cut meticulously with a hand scythe, sparing individual flowers and young seedling trees at his own discretion. If he had the necessary skills he might also deal with the hedging and ditching along the same length of road, scything in the summer and layering in the winter. Very little of this crop was wasted. The scythed grass was raked up for hay, and the hedge-trimmings

Some difficult country verges are still maintained by hand, like this one along a lane in Blythburgh, Suffolk. I like to think that this alkanet, with its beautiful sky-blue flowers, was saved by a twinge of affection from the lengthsman, and not because of the awkward proximity of that speed-restriction sign!

used for firewood.

This gentle and discriminating cutting regime, allowing the herbage to grow naturally for much of the summer, produced a sward in which a multitude of flowering plants were able to flourish, bloom and set their seed.

Hand-scything (supplemented by cutting by haymowers) continued up until at least the end of the 1950s. By then the continued increase in the length of road needing maintenance and the mounting costs of hand cutting had made it uneconomical. Therefore when powerful chemical weedkillers became available the Highways Authorities were very quick to adopt them. They were a potentially cheaper and longer-lasting alternative to cutting.

The first attempts were chiefly with dinitro compounds (DNOC). DNOC is a weedkiller which destroys plants through contact with the growing leaves. It has little effect on perennials, which include many of the most troublesome roadside weeds like couchgrass and creeping thistle, since though it kills all parts of the plant reached by the spray, it is not carried to the underground parts, which may survive to send up new shoots. It is also exceedingly poisonous to higher organisms, and will kill even quite large mammals by absorption through the skin.

The effect of the mass spraying of verges with DNOC in the late fifties was disastrous. Quite soon after spraying the foliage became as scarred and wilted as if it had been attacked by a flame-thrower. The corpses of birds and mammals unfortunate enough to be caught in the spray littered the roadsides. The devastation was so appalling that DNOC was soon withdrawn and replaced by MCPA and 2,4-D. It was a small mercy. Although vertebrate deaths were reduced, the effects on plant life were if anything even more disturbing. These hormone weedkillers work by unnaturally accelerating the growth of plants so that they literally burn themselves out. They are rapidly absorbed by all parts of the plant, leaves and roots alike, and will kill annuals and perennials, grasses and broad-leafed herbs. So in place of the parched and wilting battlefield of a few years previously, verges began to resemble sets from science-fiction horror films, covered with grotesque tangles of twisted and deformed plants.

There was a mounting public outcry against this practice, which reached one of its climaxes in Lincolnshire in 1960. One day during the summer of that year a party of botanists was visiting Tetford Hill, where the verges are scheduled as a Site of Special Scientific Interest because of their rich chalkland flora. They were shocked to find only the distorted remains of the usual mass of grassland flowers. Some local highway sprayers, looking for a site to dispose of their surplus weedkiller, had decided by a sad and thoughtless mischance to dump it on one of the finest and most attractive roadside plant communities in the county.

It is extraordinary, looking back, that these highly toxic chemicals were so indiscriminately used on such a scale without any thought being given to their possible long-term effects on the ecological and amenity value of the verges. No-one, apparently, considered the possibility that the loss of food plants along the verge might encourage both seed-eating birds and insect pests to migrate to the adjacent farmland to gorge themselves. This was a potentially much greater source of damage than drift from the sprays themselves, which the highways engineers did try to control. And some insect pests of farmland may tend to fare better when verges and hedges, which serve as base camps for many of their predators, are destroyed. A survey along a short stretch of the M1 near St Albans revealed that 67 species of insect were living in the grass. There were very few pests among them, but they did include 11 out of our 12 species of hover-fly that prey on aphids.

The situation began to be resolved by a government document which had appeared just a few years before. This was the Ministry of Transport's Circular 718 (1955), drawn up after long consultations with the Nature Conservancy and the Road Research Laboratory. Briefly, it stated that there was no objection to the use of selective weedkillers along the edges of trunk and Class 1 roads, and at certain tricky corners of Class 2 roads. It recommended spraying in May wherever possible, but that minor roads should not be managed in this way. And because of the danger of drift to nearby crops and hedgerows, spraying ought to be confined to ground within ten feet of the carriageway. Finally, it urged that stretches of road specially rich in rare or attractive plants should be spared chemical treatment completely.

Since then the use of chemical sprays has dwindled further. Total weedkillers are now rarely used outside built-up areas – or at least areas which have some sort of man-made structure on them. The edges of pavements and the feet of road signs are typical places where you may see spot or strip application of these herbicides. Selective hormone killers, like 2,4-D, are used on an even smaller scale, largely on newly seeded verges, or to control local infestations of particular weeds.

There are a number of factors which have brought about this change in attitude. Most significant is probably the increasing realisation of what a crucial role verges play in our landscape pattern. They are no less important than classic beauty spots just because we tend to take them for granted.

But there are practical considerations as well. Herbicides are expensive chemicals and their use, which can involve quite a substantial investment in men and equipment, does not necessarily cut maintenance costs. One spray, in fact, often costs as much as two cuts. Some local authorities, because of the nature of their local grasslands, have found that certain weedkillers actually increase the height of roadside vegetation. West Suffolk, which used a combination of broadleaf killer and growth retardant for a while, found that it killed off most of the attractive annual flowers and weaker perennial grasses, and simply gave the coarser grasses more room to grow. Wiltshire, working on a less fertile chalk soil with an expensively delicate growth retardant, kept their rough grasses down all right, but not the soaring costs of their maintenance programme.

In the end, as so often, it was a technological innovation that swung the balance: the flail-mower. This is a device which is attached to an ordinary agricultural tractor (see p 55). It will prune grass and hedge alike and shred the cuttings almost to the consistency of a coarse powder. It seemed initially to be the answer to the worries of both the Highways Departments and the conservationists. It was cheap, efficient and easy to use. Considerable lengths of verge could be mown by one man in a very short space of time. Unlike conventional mowers, the cutting height of the flail could be rapidly reset at different heights to suit the vegetation and terrain. And there was no dense layer of hay to smother the underlying flowers as resulted from conventional mechanical mowers.

But even this new gadget has its drawbacks. For a start it's apt to churn up small mammals and insects as thoroughly as the vegetation. The confetti-like residue that it leaves in its wake, being rapidly disposed of by earthworms and other soil animals, acts like a fine layer of compost, encouraging ever more lush growth of coarse grass. And it has to be said that local authorities haven't always been as prudent and intelligent in their use of this machine as one might have hoped. I have seen verges being close-mown every fortnight throughout the summer, sometimes with the cutter set so low that the top-soil has been scalped along with the grass.

45

And even the most conservation-minded Highways Department can often be at loss as to the best management programme to establish in its area. If the first main cut is made in early May, to save the summer flowers, the early-flowering species like cowslips won't be able to set their seeds. If it's done later, summer bloomers like poppies and vetches may be lost. If one annual cut is done at some six inches above ground level low-growing plants like daisies, lady's slipper and clovers may be smothered out. With more regular cuts at about three inches these species will flourish but the taller scabiouses, knapweeds and St John's worts will be lost.

In an ideal world the solution would be to work out a bespoke management programme for each individual verge, tailored to the particular safety needs of that road and specific demands of its indigenous flora. In fact an increasing number of counties are making such arrangements for their best verges under the guidance of local naturalists' groups. But such attention is clearly neither practical nor economic for hard-pressed local authorities, and some more general principles for verge management are needed.

The one that has emerged as the most popular is the tier or zoning system. This involves adopting a different approach for each of the different vegetation 'lanes' along the verge. In the commonest version of the system the strip of grass immediately adjacent to the carriageway is mown fairly closely two or three times a year, beginning in early or mid-May. This strip is usually between two and six feet wide, and keeping it in this condition ensures that there is no dangerous overhang into the road, and that pedestrians are able to walk along without too much difficulty.

On wider verges the whole width of the verge will be mown once or twice a year, often with the cutter set rather higher. This cut is usually done at the end of the growing season some time between late July and September. But occasionally there is a preliminary cut between late May and early July. The scrubby back-layer may be left altogether, or tackled where necessary along with the hedging in winter.

If there is only time and manpower for one cut per year, cutting the whole width of the verge in late May will keep visibility satis-

The tier system of mowing on a minor road in Buckinghamshire, early May

factory on most roads and save the best of the summer-flowering plants.

Theoretically, the tier system has the advantages of producing a verge that is safe, pleasant to look at, ecologically diverse and cheap to maintain. How has it worked out in practice?

J. M. Way's pamphlet, *Road Verges on Rural Roads*, by far the most comprehensive account of modern verge management, describes at least eighteen variations on the tier system across the country, depending on the timing of the cuts and the widths of verge mown at each cut. Often these variations are the result of particular local problems, or the county's budget. But they are also influenced by just how much weight the Highways Department gives to amenity considerations. Although Dr Way found that 'amenity' rated only second to safety in the table of management priorities, it is plainly a very subjective notion, open to many different interpretations. These are some of the edited comments he recorded on the importance of amenity as a reason for management. The number of counties expressing the same view, where more than one, are in brackets.

Requirements vary with the place (2); only in built-up areas; the most important reason (5); not a county problem (8); tidiness, not wildflowers, no public pressure for wildflowers (8); encourage spring flowers (2); appearance and amenity includes 'weeds'; pride in neat and tidy appearance (3); ditto, especially where there are tourists (4); not a parks department – amenity cutting kept to a minimum; aim to keep as natural as possible in rural areas; pressure from urban people coming to live in the country to keep verges tidy; country people complaining about untidy verges; country people complaining about loss of wildflowers; avoid disturbance to pheasants' nests (5); farmers want on verges what (wildflowers, etc) they have lost in their fields.

In East Suffolk, where there are over 4,000 miles of verge, the County Surveyor has translated the system into the following management plan:

At the beginning of the 'grass season' all verges are cut one width, ie 3ft to 4ft from the edge of the carriageway, plus all sight lines, visibility splays, etc. In a normal season, with the resources available, this cycle is achieved before the grass is ready to be cut again. The aim is to cut all verges in this continuous cyclic manner between two and three times per season. In addition, an attempt is made to cut the whole verge before the end of the season, if weather, breakdowns, etc, permits. [In correspondence with the author.]

The shortage of manpower and equipment is a constant worry to the Highways Departments. West Suffolk's system, for instance, is basically the same as the East's, but:

In earlier years we found that in cutting the verges on the trunk and main roads first in the season with the equipment and labour available, the growth on the minor roads could often become a real problem. Some four years ago (1968) it was decided to spray by contract the verges on approximately 120 miles of the trunk and principal roads with grass inhibitor so that the cutters could be deployed on the minor roads straightaway at the beginning of the season. This has enabled us to keep the growth of the verges reasonably well under control. Only 3 to 6 feet of the 120 miles of main road verges were sprayed and, of course none of the verges of special interest. (See p 51.) [In correspondence with the author.]

Dr E. M. Buckle of the Settle and District Civic Society, who surveyed the verge-management programmes of forty authorities in 1971, found that over 80 per cent expressed interest in the conservation of verge flora, provided this didn't conflict with road safety. Most followed the tier-system in some form, though there was great variety in the details of the schemes. In Devon 'verges where colonies of wild flowers flourish are not cut until after the flowering season'. In Northumberland, where they only mow the first six feet of verge regularly, 'the remaining portion, in all cases except on trunk roads, will give wild flowers the opportunity of growing, as this area is only cut once a year on principal roads, every two years on class two and heavily trafficated class three roads, and every other year on all other roads.'

A most encouraging development is the number of Highways Departments that are co-operating with local naturalists' groups to ensure the conservation of outstanding stretches of verge. In Dorset, the Roads and Bridges Department works in conjunction with the Dorset Naturalists' Trust, the County Planning Office, the Council for the Preservation of Rural England and the Nature Conservancy. In Derbyshire, the County Council has a Countryside Sub-Committee, on which the County Naturalists' Trust is represented.

These agreements aren't simply gestures to the whims of a few botanists. Many authorities are just as concerned with the appeal of the verges to the general public. Northumberland's Highways Committee agreed to a request by the Northumberland and Durham Naturalists' Trust to give certain stretches of verge special attention on account of '(a) their scientific interest for biologists; (b) their aesthetic value for the general public. Other verges were to be cut judiciously, to maintain the maximum aesthetic and biological interest and still produce the necessary conditions of safety for all road-users.'

Some of these verges are actually designated as nature reserves and marked-up for the benefit of the mowing gangs. Cornwall indicates its star-rated verges with plain wooden posts. So does Kent, where these simple and sympathetic instructions are given to local surveyors: 'Verges having botanical interest: please have these verges in your division marked by chestnut spiles painted white at the top six inches. Spiles must mark each end of the area concerned.' Oxfordshire has wired off a few of its richest patches (particularly if they contain orchids) to keep out rabbits as well as to alert the mowers.

One of the best examples of co-operation occurs in the Breckland. In many places, road verges are the last relics of this extraordinary sandy waste that once covered nearly 400 square miles of East Anglia. Breckland has a unique collection of plants, some of which grow nowhere else in the British Isles and belong really to the Russian steppes. It was not surprising, therefore, that as the sandy fields and heaths began to be swallowed up by conifer plantations, the Nature Conservancy took steps to preserve whatever remnants of this habitat they could. In consultation with the Suffolk Trust for Nature Conservation and the County Surveyor of West Suffolk they drew up schedules for the management of a score of Breckland verges over about twenty miles of road.

The following table gives full descriptions of some of these verges, and the prescribed systems of management. The County Surveyor of West Suffolk tells me that, so far, these mowing regimes have presented no problems, either in terms of manpower, cost, or safety, and they adhere scrupulously to the suggested schemes.

50

*(B = both sides   N, S, E, W = north, south, east, west)

Ref. No.	Locality	Road	N.G.R.	Length (m)	*Position	Description	Prescribed Management
1	Cherry Hill, Barton Mills	C71 U22	TL720722 to TL730719 TL721714 to TL723726	2,300	B	Probably best verges in Breck. Chiefly grassland species: many rarities.	Cut before mid-May and after late September.
2	Cavenham	U17	TL760704 to TL768713	1,200	B	Relic heathland verges with both chalk and acid grassland species present.	Cut before mid-May and after late September.
3	Tuddenham	C12	TL743711 to TL751709	800	S	A mixed verge of chalk-loving species.	Cut before mid-May and after late September.
4	Tuddenham Cavenham Heath NNR	U18	TL745722 to TL758728	1,500	B	On either side of track running through Cavenham Heath NNR for integral part of surrounding heath flora.	No cutting required.
5	Chalk Hill, Barton Mills	A11	TL705715 to TL710724	600	B	Road widening recently has bared underlying chalk and rapid colonisation by chalk-loving species has occurred.	Requires scrub clearance along east bank of south lane of dual carriageway.
6	Icklingham	B1112	TL768734 to TL766738	600	B	Mixed chalk and sandy acid grassland.	Cut before mid-May and after late September.
11	Rampart Field, West Stow	C74	TL786715 to TL730768	300	B	Continuous with Rampart Field and although heavily used by public, still has interesting heath flora.	Cut before mid-May and after late September.
12	Kings Forest, West Stow	C74	TL804713 to TL812709	900	B	Show some relics of flora that once covered the now afforested West Stow Heath.	Cut before mid-May and after late September.
13	Warren House, Euston	A1088	TL894796 to TL893802	700	W	Small area of acid grass heath, bordering verges have similar flora.	Cut before mid-June and after July.
14	Barnham Barracks, Barnham	A134	TL863803 to TL864808	500	W	Continuous with Barnham Cross Common (Norfolk). Several interesting heathland plants.	Cut before mid-May and after late September.
15	Thetford Heath, Barnham	C31	TL840797 to TL857794	1,800	B	Possesses relic of heathland flora with both chalk and acid grassland species.	One cut late September.
16	Horn and Weather Heath, Elveden	A11	TL782883 to TL788776	650	B	Wide verges bordering Horn and Weather Heath SSSI. Of interest as possess some of components of neighbouring Heaths.	Cut before June and after July.
17	Mile End, Brandon	A1065	TL774855 to TL776858	300	S	Although heavily disturbed in places by parked cars and lorries, are still important site for Breckland rarity, Field Southernwood.	Cut before mid-May and after late September.

From *Transactions of the Suffolk Naturalists' Society* (January 1971)

A stretch of verge along Cherry Hill, at Barton Mills in the Breckland (Ref No 1 in the table on page 51). It is impossible to do justice to the beauty of this verge in black and white, but you can see the very fine quality of the grass, which harbours a huge range of low-flowering species. I took this photo in late June and there must have been something like a hundred species in flower along the half-mile stretch I studied, including cypress spurge, Breckland catchfly (a member of the campion family with sticky stems that do indeed catch flies, but for no apparent purpose), flixweed, wild thyme, evening primrose, mignonette, viper's bugloss, hound's tongue and Scotch thistle.

There are now over forty scheduled verges in the county for which management schemes have been agreed with the County Surveyors. The Suffolk Trust for Nature Conservation has also launched two schemes for wardening further stretches. The first, put forward in 1970, invited members of the county's Women's Institutes to report to the Trust on any verges which carried interesting or attractive communities of flowers, or even unusual individual specimens. The Trust would then discuss with the Nature

Conservancy what action should be taken, and bring in the County Council to discuss the most appropriate management scheme. The follow-up would be equally important, and people living in the area would be asked to report each summer on the way the management was actually being carried out on the ground.

In 1973, the Trust began a project to map the county's roadside flora more comprehensively. Members with a certain amount of botanical expertise were invited to keep an eye on one or more 10km squares in the county, to observe whether the cutting of protected stretches was being carried out according to the agreed plan, and to report any departures from the plan. And they were also asked to assist with the maintenance of marker posts along scheduled verges, and to report any new sites which might be worthy of protection to the Trust's Conservation Officer. If a new site looks a likely – and practicable – candidate for protection, the individual who put in the recommendation will be sent a map of the relevant 10km square, and be asked to mark the exact position of the site and the length of verge which would need protection. The maximum amount of information on the plant species present is also needed at this stage.

One of the greatest hopes for the conservation of our countryside lies in local vigilante systems of this sort. There is no reason why any individual, school or local natural history society should not initiate schemes similar to those operating in Suffolk. Your County Conservation Trust will be delighted to receive reports of verges that you consider worthy of special protection. The recommendation should be as detailed as possible, and should include a map reference, as full a list of the resident plants as you can compile, and whatever knowledge you have of the current mowing arrangements. And while you are about it, send a copy of your letter to the County Surveyor. He is unlikely to initiate any special protection measures without advice from the Trust, but it's important that he is constantly reminded about public interest in roadside flowers.

Hedges

It wouldn't be difficult to argue that the hedgerow is the most distinctive feature of the British rural scene. Although the majority of our hedges date from no earlier than the eighteenth and nineteenth century Parliamentary Enclosures, nothing seems more typical of the ancient pattern of our landscape than a patchwork of fields stitched together by these strips of hawthorn, hazel and elm. No wonder that their wholesale destruction by farmers over the last twenty years, however necessary it has seemed economically, has caused such bitterness and worry amongst country-lovers.

Roadside hedges are in essence no different to those that run through the interior of farms, and it would be presumptuous to try to add here to the immense amount that has already been written about the importance of these hedges to our wildlife. But although hedges are, strictly speaking, the responsibility of the owners of the land they border, those that adjoin roads are usually maintained with at least as much thought for road safety and 'tidiness' as for agricultural convenience. So there are things we can say about them that are within the province of this book.

By and large roadside hedges have probably fared rather better than those 'inland'. Being absolute boundaries to a field, and therefore presenting no real obstruction to the movement of big agricultural machines, there are fewer reasons for their being uprooted altogether. Some farmers even look on them benignly as useful barriers for keeping the picnicking public out of their wheat. Farmers are also likely to be rather more careful about setting fire to them during stubble and straw burning – from fear of possible legal repercussions, if nothing else. In the summer of 1973, there was a twenty-car pile-up on the M1 as a result of smoke blown over the motorway from a particularly reckless piece of field-burning.

So roadside hedges probably represent a fairly small proportion of the 5,000 miles of hedge that are estimated to be lost from our countryside every year. But those that do survive are often emaciated shadows of their old selves. The demands of good drainage and road safety can mean that hedges are kept in a state of permanent stuntedness, often scarcely able to flower and set fruit, let alone grow into vaguely natural shapes.

The flail-mower, ironically, has been one of the greatest villains here. With its cutter simply set vertically instead of horizontally, the flail can shred through branches up to two inches thick, reducing

Flail-mower at work near Blythburgh, Suffolk. This piece of hedge-mangling was done in the last week of May only twenty yards across the road from a national nature reserve. One pair of nightingales deserted their nest in this hedge almost immediately afterwards.

Flail-mown hedge at Hinton, East Suffolk

the whole outer growth of the hedge to splinters and wood pulp. I don't think I know any more heartbreaking sight in the country-side than a hedge which has been wrecked by deep cutting with a flail. It puts the problem of 'vandalism' very firmly in perspective. The mashed and split ends of the branches leave a rash of white scars along the hedge for the whole year, and the bushes wide open to attack by fungus and disease. Although most hedge-cutting is supposed to be done during the winter, it is increasingly spreading into the summer, when birds are nesting and the shrubs are in flower.

Hedges, except where they have been planted on highway land by a council, are the responsibility of the adjoining landowner. The Highways Department is not obliged – or indeed entitled – to manage them, except where the hedges present a safety hazard. But different councils approach this situation very differently. Many have reached working relationships with some of the hedge-owners, and do their cutting for them. Even where there is no such agreement, councils will often control the encroachment of woody growth onto their verges, and trim up the face and top of the hedge.

It's a shame that hedging is administered in such a haphazard way. If it could be laid down that the Highways Department was always legally responsible for the maintenance of the road-facing side of the hedge, we might be able to develop management programmes – satisfactory to farmers, motorists and conservationists alike – comparable to those that are evolving for grass verges.

The style of management of a hedge, as with most habitats, is one of the chief factors in determining how popular it is with wildlife. An old and gently-managed hedge supports an astonishing range of plants and animals. Just about every species of native British tree and shrub, and a good number of introduced species, can be found somewhere along our hedgerows. The older the hedge the greater the number of species. Where it is a remnant of the natural forest rather than a deliberately planted boundary, there may be mature woodland trees — oak, ash, holly and elm. The elms are a marvellously varied collection themselves, contributing perhaps more than any other single family to the regional flavour of old hedgerows: the common English elm of the south and Midlands, with its classic rounded top; the more spacious wych elms of the north and west; the shorter and finer-twigged small-leaved elms of East Anglia, and the slender Cornish elm with its upturned branches. On the Midlands plain, hawthorn is the commonest hedgerow species and in the Home Counties also blackthorn and hazel. There are broom hedges in East Suffolk, gorse banks in Pembrokeshire and naturalised fuchsias in the west of Ireland. The richest hedges are probably on chalk country where there may be a wealth of flowering and berry-bearing shrubs – privet, box, dogwood, yew, wayfaring tree, cherry and whitebeam. And through all these hedges there may be climbers like ivy, honeysuckle and bramble.

In the undergrowth you may find hedgehogs, bank voles, shrews, wood and yellow-necked mice; insect-eating birds foraging amongst the leaf litter; flowers like campions, celandines, bluebells and ground ivy. Hedge garlic whose spruce white flowers are one of the first to appear in the spring, supports the caterpillars of orange-tip and green-veined white butterflies. Even nettles play their part by providing food for peacock and small tortoiseshell caterpillars. The fully-fledged butterflies, plus bees, hoverflies and a multitude of other insects, enjoy flying around in the still air under the lee of a hedge, and help in their turn to pollinate the low-flowering plants. And in this dense herbage nest partridges, pheasants, larks, whitethroats and willow warblers.

In the bottom branches of the hedge there are different species – wrens and yellowhammers weave their nests amongst the tangle of ivy-clad roots and rough grasses a foot or so above the ground. Higher still there will be blackbirds, thrushes, dunnocks and chaffinches – and even more insects. The leaves of our most widespread hedgerow bush, the hawthorn, provide food for many species of moth, including the winter, vapourer and green-brindled crescent. At the very top of the tallest hedges the species are fewer, but there may still be a magpie's nest or squirrel's drey, and even some of those seemingly earth-bound mice and voles tightrope-walking along the twigs after the haws.

Where mature oaks are part of the hedge there is a habitat in which 500 species of insect have been found and 20 species of bird known to nest, including woodland species like owls, nuthatches and woodpeckers.

But technology has caught up with the hedgerow oaks. Until recently their sheer bulk and stubborn strength meant that they were often grudgingly left alone whilst the hedges around them were torn out. Needless to say such obstinacy in the face of progress could not be tolerated, and a new piece of murderous equipment was developed, the hydraulic tree lift. Attached to the back of a tractor this works like a giant pair of dentist's pincers, and can draw out a troublesome tree a few hundred years old in about four minutes flat.

It is tragic that we should be losing trees deliberately like this. Oaks are already disappearing from our countryside at the rate of

100,000 a year, as a result of old age, disease, pollution, reafforestation with conifers and so on. Only three saplings of our most famous and ecologically rich tree are planted for every hundred lost, and seedlings which regenerate naturally from fallen acorns are quickly put paid to by the flail.

How is the rest of that remarkable wildlife community, the hedgerow, making do under modern management techniques?

A hedge was layered perhaps every seven years by bending over the thin trunks of the growing bushes almost parallel to the ground, and weaving them around stakes driven into the ground every yard or so. The top of the hedge was crowned by a tightly woven layer of shoots (hethers) which prevented the growing branches springing erect. Surplus twigs and branches were lopped off altogether.

For the first couple of years after layering, this kind of hedge was a fairly thinly populated habitat, and at no time would it be allowed to attain the height and thickness needed by many species of hedge bird. But it quickly developed a rich ground flora, with

Hedge layering in Leicestershire. A rare sight anywhere, now that hedges can be kept in trim more simply, quickly and cheaply by mechanical means

all the accompanying insects and birds, and it would invariably be studded with a selection of full-grown trees and shrubs – a good cropping hazel-nut, a horse chestnut to give shelter for horses and cattle – which were spared at the hedger's discretion. Flail-mowers, unfortunately, can't tell the difference between an elder and an elm.

A steep West Country hedgebank, one of the richest hedge types. Very rich ground flora, including ferns and mosses, and dense hedge bottom

The A-shape, perhaps the closest modern equivalent to the layered hedge. It's not trimmed with a flail mower, but with a more conventional type of hedge-cutter.

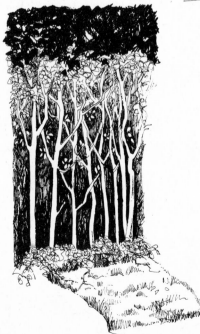

The wasp-waisted hedge produced by a flail-mower cutting deep into a tall hedge is little good to man or beast. Apart from its unsightliness it has virtually no thickness at the bottom, and little ground flora because of shade from the overhang.

The kind of hedge which develops maybe a score of years after a quickset hedge is planted and allowed to grow unchecked. Good to look at, it will invariably contain bird-sown shrubs of other species like cherry and blackthorn as well as the may. A good nesting ground for blackbirds and magpies, but little ground flora because of the shade

The flowering shrubs of the hedgerow are one of the delights of our lanes, and one that you can appreciate even whilst you are moving. Their blossoms are a litany of profuse and delicate colour right through the year, from the yellow clouds of pussy willow in early March through to the mute green but sweet-smelling ivy flowers which may stay on the vine till early winter. Their magic was caught wonderfully by H. E. Bates, in his essay 'The Woods in Spring':

The delicate flowers and catkins of the hazel. If these are destroyed by flailing in the spring, the bush will not produce nuts

How is it that this current of cream and white and pink goes on and on through the wild trees of England almost without break or variation? The chestnut and the crab and the wild rose and even the blackberry are white and pink. The dogwood and the elder and the lime are cream. The rest are white. And all are scented, either with that summery faintness of the may or with the absolute pure sweetness of the crab and the chestnut and the rose. We have no wild exotic blossoming tree of scarlet or blue or purple. There is a sort of Northern delicacy, almost fragility, about them all. The flames of the chestnut candelabra burn sweetly and quietly, many little flames of softest pink in the white cups of wax above the drooping clusters of seven leaves. The rose has no passion, only that immeasurable and matchless sweetness that fills the hot days of June and July as the heavenliness of the lime drenches the summer nights.

from H. E. Bates, *Through the Woods* (1936)

63

There are some places, though, where even the best of hedges would be a blot on the landscape. The Manifold Valley, Derbyshire

Hedgerow Snacks

If you pesire more practical rewards from the hedgerows than these, you will be pleased to know that something like twenty-five species of edible berry can be found along our roadsides. Blackberries and crab apples (good for jelly if a little sour raw) need no introduction. But the fact that the wild ancestors of the raspberry, gooseberry, pear and blackcurrant grow wild in our hedges may be less well known. They look the same as their cultivated descendants and, for those who don't object to a little tanginess in their food, are just as flavoursome.

REMEMBER THAT BLACKBERRY JAM
WE MADE TOGETHER LAST YEAR?

OUR BIRDS AND SMALL WILD CREATURES NEED
THE SHELTER AND FOOD OF THE HEDGEROWS—
THAT'S WHY WE ASK THE FARMER TO SPARE
AS MANY HEDGES AS HE CAN, BESIDES........

YOU CAN'T PICK BLACKBERRIES FROM A BARBED-WIRE FENCE!

European Conservation Year 1970

Less easily recognised are the whitebeam and the now scarce barberry. The berries of the former hang in orange-red clusters from a tree whose leaves are flashed with silver on the undersides. They're hardly palatable when raw, but when the fruits have gone rotten – 'bletted' – they're quite pleasant to eat with honey. Barberries were exterminated in many hedges by farmers after it was found that they harboured a wheat parasite. But you may still find the odd spiny specimen, with its clusters of oblong, scarlet berries. They make a good jelly, or can be dried or pickled as an accompaniment to curries.

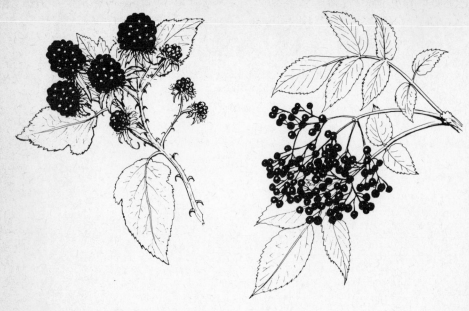

Blackberries and elderberries

There are some curious superstitions about the dire effects of eating many of our hedgerow fruits. Elderberries won't upset your stomach even if eaten raw, provided they're picked fully-ripe, when the umbels of fruit have turned upside down. But they're best added to blackberry and apple pies, or simmered gently with vinegar and spices, when they make a kind of fruity Worcestershire sauce.

Rowanberries, from the mountain ash, are as common planted along urban roads as in country hedges. You won't be popular with either the council or the town thrushes if you start picking their orange fruits. But there are always plenty blown down by the wind in the autumn. If you gather these up and wash them well they make a superb, smoky, marmalade-coloured jelly to serve with lamb or game.

The fruit of the blackthorn gives its flavour and brilliant purple colour to sloe gin, and rose-hips are made into the famous syrup.

Even haws aren't unpleasant. Personally, I think they should be left to help the birds through the lean winter months. But if you fancy nibbling the odd one, the flesh round the central stone is not unlike under-ripe avocado pear.

But if you aren't tempted by these wild oddities, there are often cultivated fruit trees to be found along roadsides, sprung perhaps, in a neat cycle, from the remnants of picnickers' desserts. Fruit for free by the wayside can include wild apples, bullaces, damsons, and even that relic of the medieval garden, the medlar.

Traveller's Trees
There are flowers and shrubs in our hedgerows that earned a special place in the affection of early travellers. As with the plants of sheep country, their reward was a name. They became the botanical mascots of footweary wayfarers. Traveller's joy is the best known and one of the oldest named. This wild clematis, which can drape hedgerows on chalky soil like a tangle of liana, had a host of ancient and functional titles: bedwind in Dorset, boy's

Traveller's joy on a chalk bank in the Chilterns

bacca in Hampshire, shepherd's delight in Somerset, old man's beard everywhere. It was not until 1597 that the herbalist John Gerard, always felicitous at naming, added traveller's joy to the list:

This plant is commonly called *Viorna, Quasi Vias Ornans*, of decking and adorning waies and hedges, where people travel; and there upon I have named it the Traveller's Joy.

These plants have no use in physic as yet found, but are esteemed only for pleasure, by reason of the goodly shadow which they make with their thicke bushing and clyming, as also for the beauty of the floures, and the pleasant sent or savour of the same.

from *The Herball*

The name stuck, and I suspect not just because of the shelter sunstruck walkers could find under 'the goodly shadow' its branches. In November and December, its feathery white fruits are a sight to see cascading over the barren winter hedges. Deeper still into winter the dry stems were cut for smoking – hence boy's bacca, shepherd's delight, poor man's friend.

But it's been an immemorial rule of the road that one traveller's joy is another's misfortune, and on the continent professional beggars used to employ old man's beard in one of their sharper practices. The juice of the leaves was rubbed into scratches on the skin, raising large superficial sores and giving the user an appearance miserable enough to con alms out of the most hard-hearted wayfarer.

Ground elder was also goutweed and herb Gerard – the herb of the patron saint of the gouty. It was introduced by the Romans as a vegetable and a medicinal herb for gout and sciatica; also 'joint-aches and other cold griefs' – custom-built for all the ills of the intemperate traveller in fact. So it was planted in the physic gardens of wayside inns and from there has spread along much of our road system by means of those tenaciously aggressive roots that so enrage modern gardeners.

Ground elder, or herb Gerard

Then there is the wayfaring tree, another common shrub of chalk hedgerows. This too could give shelter – to a short or prostrate traveller. But most likely it got its name from the delightful and heavily fragrant cream blossoms which stud the shrub in May.

Lastly, if you should want a floral St Christopher, a plant to carry with you, there is the speedwell, a roadside plant which would speed you on your way. In Ireland, where it was also called wish-me-well, it was sewn on the clothes of travellers to guard them from accidents.

Ditches

Hedging and ditching have always gone together, and still much of the most drastic cutting back of wayside hedges is done to prevent their young growth and leaf-fall clogging up drainage dykes. It's overdone more often than not, with the flail-mower taking out the whole of one side of the hedge, instead of just the over-hanging branches and the runners actually emerging inside the ditch. But the alternative may be worse. The government offers a grant of 60 per cent for installing piped drains and the sealing up of ditches. Since the result needs no maintenance either by the landowner or the Highways Department, it's an offer which is readily snapped up, and all over the countryside you will see those tunnels under hedgerows being filled in – often with alien soil. Where ditches are retained, they're often mechanically maintained with dragline excavators. The result is a sharp V-shaped profile, not the gentle U of the hand-dug dyke, and with no real floor there's little chance of the ditch developing any marsh-like qualities.

But is there that much value in a ditch? If the coming of piped drainage reduces the need for such drastic crew-cutting of hedges isn't it all to the good? This might be so if the remainder of the wet places in our countryside weren't in such a perilous state. Marshes and fens are being drained, farm ponds filled in, rivers almost dried up by our colossal consumption of water. We would not normally think of classing ditches with these respectable habitats; the very word rings with disrespect and muckiness. Yet a decent-sized ditch, particularly one dug out to service the run-off from the adjacent fields as well as the road, can carry miniaturised versions of all these habitats. It will be marshy for much of its length, and for much of the year; pond-like in the deeper and wider sections and carrying running water after heavy rain and snow. I can't think of very much of the commoner wetland wildlife that I've not seen at some time or another in ditches. Moorhens nest in them; so do reed buntings and sedge warblers if there is sufficient scrub. I've watched a migrant black tern quartering a wide roadside dyke in north Norfolk for a whole afternoon, herons fishing in reedy ditches and snipe jinking up from muddy ones. In the wetter dykes there are likely to be frogs and toads as well as water voles. If a ditch links up with a nearby river, there may be eels too.

Which is to say nothing about ditch flowers. In some areas ditches may be literally the only sites available for wetland plants like marsh marigolds, yellow iris and great willow herb.

It is a formidable collection to wipe out at a stroke. And it is not just that closing the ditch wipes out a whole community –

The yellow flag, our commonest wild iris – though it may be the original of the French fleur-de-lis lily emblem. Most distinguished of all ditch flowers, it is ablaze with huge golden blooms from June to August.

water, wetland plants, the insects that live on them and support, in their turn, the birds. It changes the whole character of the adjoining verge. Without damp and irrigation some of the shrubs and plant species will vanish altogether. So too will the sunny embankments of the ditch itself, still one of the best sites for roadside primroses.

Ditch-Dipping

If a roadside ditch is old and broad enough it's likely to develop some of the same animal and insect life as a pond. You can go dipping for these with a net and jam jar just as you would in a pond. What you find will not only be fascinating in its own right, but an indicator of the condition of the ditch.

Very shallow dykes that are likely to dry up completely in the summer and freeze solid in the winter will carry a rather restricted collection of those animals that are able to cope with these extreme conditions. Water fleas and fairy shrimps, which produce drought-resistant eggs, newts which move onto the land anyway for much

This ditch in Wenhaston, Suffolk is one of the healthy ones, catching the run-off from the adjacent marshland as well as the road. In the summer it's frothy with meadowsweet blossom and, where there's room, water figwort, fleabane and spearwort. In the winter I've seen kingfishers flying over this stretch and once a water rail mincing through the rushes.

of their lives, and water boatmen and water beetles which migrate to other open water if a ditch dries out will be found.

Stickleback Gasterosteus aculeatus

Dytiscus larva Dytiscus marginalis

Water boatman Notonecta glauca

In streams and rivers it's possible to estimate how polluted the water is from the animals which live in it. This is more difficult with still water, as the natural decay of waterplants and fallen leaves depletes the oxygen in precisely the same way as man-made organic pollutants. There are certain water animals which can tolerate these conditions, and if you find them in large numbers in a ditch it's likely either to be polluted or choked with a great deal of dead vegetation. Most of these animals are scavengers which feed on bacteria and other products of decay and which have special adaptations to these rough conditions. Blood-worms contain oxygen-preserving haemoglobin (just like our own bodies) and can survive in badly de-oxygenated water. Mosquito larvae and rat-tailed maggots take in air from the surface through breathing tubes.

The richest ditches are the wide, open ones which receive a good deal of sunlight, and aren't overhung by foliage. These may contain water snails, mayfly, caddis fly and dragonfly larvae, water skaters sculling on the surface and water boatman underneath.

Caddis fly larva Mystacides azurea

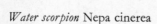

Water scorpion Nepa cinerea

Great pond snail Limnaea stagnalis

Water crowfoot Ranunculus aquatilis

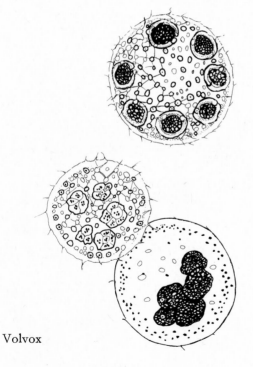

Volvox

(Upside down incidentally – a reminder that for many water creatures the air is the element to dip into!) Preying on these may be sticklebacks and the voraciously carnivorous great diving beetle, which is quite likely to give *you* a nip if you put your hand in the net.

Perhaps most fascinating of all are *volvox*, which are colonies of microscopic plants shaped like the trappings of a planetarium – stars and spheres and satellites. They are never much bigger than pinheads, so you will need a good magnifying glass to appreciate their structures.

One final point. Do return all your catches very gently to the ditch once you have finished studying them.

Roadside dykes and ponds can also be important breeding grounds for the common toad, one of those species that breed colonially in the same site for generations. But it is an unlucky colony that finds itself in such a site, adjacent to a road, for twice a year they are going to have to negotiate a crossing.

Toads are migratory animals. They spawn in water, but hibernate through the winter on land, holed up in cellars, rabbit warrens, compost heaps and flower pots. When the spring rains come they begin their laborious crawl back to their ancient breeding

Pair of dead common toads

Toad rescue seems to be spreading. This sixteen-year-old Hertfordshire schoolboy was taking part in 'Operation Toad Lift' organised by the Hertfordshire and Middlesex Trust for Nature Conservation on roads near a set of gravel pits at Bourne End. Volunteers weren't hard to find, given the toad's reputation as a friendly and voracious muncher of garden pests. With the help of buckets and torches a magnificent total of 1,300 toads were ferried to safety by the end of April.

sites. It's probable that some of these have been in use for centuries, long before the roads were even built, let alone used by motor traffic. But when the roads did come they inevitably crossed the toads' traditional cross-country migratory routes, from which the toads, being conservative creatures, would not be shifted.

With instincts and preferences that are beyond our understanding, they will still head resolutely towards their home-water in late March and April, sometimes travelling as much as a mile from their hibernation sites, oblivious to other ponds and dykes on the way, and to the dangers of the roads across their path.

It is pitiful to see them on this stage of their journey, their delicate amphibious feet scarcely able to cope with the hard and slippery asphalt. They can take over ten minutes to cross a narrow country lane.

Some friends who live near the north Norfolk coastal marshes organise toad crossing patrols around the time of the spring migrations. On wet days they go out during the evening rush hour (if any hour in rural Norfolk can be called rushed), hold up the traffic and ferry the toads gently across the road on shovels.

But here, as everywhere, hundreds are still slaughtered. Some are caught, pathetically, like the pair in the photo on p 77, attempting to mate on the journey. On a quarter-mile stretch of the unclassified East Suffolk road where I took this picture I counted over 180 corpses after one particularly rainy night in April.

Roadside furniture

Man-made furniture sprouts by the roadside as luxuriantly as hedges and trees – and a good deal more luxuriantly in places: milestones (good for lichens); a disused horse trough carrying a few inches of rain for birds to bathe in; fences; cavernous old-style street-lights and moth-drawing sodium lamps. The crossroads gibbet has disappeared but it has a natural successor in those admonitory road safety posters.

But these days the most distinctive adornments are the poles and cables of the telephone system, run along the road edge, like so many other services, for ease of access and to interfere as little as possible with farmland.

The more adaptable creatures haven't been slow to cash in on these structures. Creosoted wood and brick walls may not contribute much to the food-cycle – though I've seen a green woodpecker hammering at a telegraph pole, and have no doubt that scavenging

Little Owl

kites and crows had a thoroughly mercenary interest in those wayside gibbets – but they can provide for most of a bird's furniture needs. Tits, starlings and sparrows nest in old-fashioned lamp standards and sometimes feed late into the night on the insects attracted by the light and warmth. The hole left by a missing stone in a wall may be commandeered by a pair of wheatears or redstarts.

But it is in providing perches, look-outs and song posts that roadside furniture makes its special contribution. It can even be preferable to natural vegetation for this purpose if it's not screened by foliage. For a hunting bird an uninterrupted view is worth sacrificing a little cover for. Indeed, your best chance of seeing little owls and buzzards close-to is when they are hunched at the top of a telegraph pole waiting for a vole or rabbit to come into the open. It may be a lazy way of hunting, but not such an ineffective one if you happen to be shaped and coloured like a short log.

In many of the treeless wastes of central France shrikes will only be found along those strips, often by road-sides, where telegraph wires or high fences provide a look-out post. Some shrikes have even been observed going one stage further and using the spikes along a barbed wire fence as artificial thorns for impaling their prey.

But one adaptation still remains a mystery. What did swallows do before the Post Office wired up our villages with thousands of miles of artificial perch? In late summer, as they line up restlessly shoulder to shoulder before the arduous journey home, it is difficult to think how they could manage these gatherings on anything other than telegraph wires. Yet writing in the early 1880s, only ten years before the telephone system was opened, Richard Jefferies saw them making do in other ways:

> The swallows, too, are not without thought of going. They may be seen twenty in a row, one above the other, on the slanting ropes of guys which hold up the masts of the rickcloths over the still unfinished cornricks. They gather in rows on the ridges of the tiles, and wisely take counsel of each other.
>
> from *Nature near London*

Roofs and rickcloths – to discover a natural forebear of the telegraph wire, the swallows' ancestral migratory perch, we would need to go back to the time when they preferred to nest in caves rather than barns.

Swallows do make the summer, and it is one of the glimmers of hope in the endless story of destruction and exile in our countryside that a bird like this should choose to breed and 'take counsel' on man-made furniture rather than natural.

LABOUR-SAVING

A kestrel was hovering over the grass verge of a road through the Mendips. It hung motionless, head to wind, with the claws of one foot negligently hooked round a telegraph wire, about midway between two poles; the other foot was half retracted. Thus supported by the breeze and anchored by the wire, which was raised several inches above its normal position, the bird had no need of frequent wing-beats to remain in place.

Note from John E. Platt in The Countryman

Corn bunting

One of the mysteries surrounding the corn bunting is why its distribution should be so patchy. It never breeds far away from open areas of cultivated land, yet you may pass from one such area where the birds seem to be singing from every fence and bush to another, apparently identical, where they are completely absent. The availability of song posts may be a factor, though in some barren areas in Scotland they seem to be quite happy with a foot or two of dried flower-stalk. But there's little doubt that where they're available, overhead telegraph wires are by far the most favoured perches.

I always associate the corn bunting with parched July days in chalk country. It drones out its rattling song interminably through the heat, and one patient ornithologist counted 338 songs almost without break in the space of a single hour. Yet the downland landscape would not be the same without this dry jangle, which seems utterly a part of the haze and the open corn.

The corn bunting is a drab, slothful bird, so ungainly in the breeding season that its legs dangle as it flies. Yet it has a certain dignity, keeping patient vigil over its territory from the wires.

This enterprising great tit nested successfully 2 feet down in one of the hollow support posts of the village boundary sign in Ringshall, Buckinghamshire.

Starlings congregating for roosting

(right) Male wheatear bringing food to a nest in a roadside wall in Yorkshire

(below) Wall pennywort on a dry-stone wall in Pembrokeshire

85

PART TWO

ENTER THE CAR

Bulldozers at work on M5 construction

Mixed blessing

If we look at roads simply as tracks through the countryside they clearly go some way towards compensating for the forest and farmland they eat up by adding variety and interest to the landscape. They open up what would often be impenetrable and unviewable country. They help conserve our dwindling stock of grassland. Along their hedges and verges wildlife can commute as freely as humans on the road surface.

Indeed it would be possible to wind up our look at the wildlife of roads here and now if what passed along them was still nothing more than a slow trickle of cattle and walkers. With such a modest and gentle traffic all roads could have developed into natural communities as stable as old downland.

But human evolution proceeds at a breakneck pace, and the dominant species on roads now is not *homo ambulans* but *homo vehicularis* – predatory, aggressive, fast-moving, territorially expansive and multiplying faster than a promiscuous rabbit. There never can have been such a mixed blessing in the countryside as the motor vehicle. It has probably been indirectly – and in many cases directly – responsible for more damage than any other single force; yet it has also opened people's eyes to just what a precious and vulnerable landscape it is threatening.

Much of the rest of this book is taken up with cataloguing the devastation wrought by the car on the natural communities of the road. I feel it's only fair, therefore, to begin with some tribute to what the car has done for the countryside, and particularly for the people that move about in it and enjoy it.

My own feelings may or may not be typical. I have no particular affection for cars. I don't like what they do to their drivers any more than what they do to the countryside. I deliberately lived without one for ten years, and did not think it too hypocritical to cadge lifts remorselessly from my friends. At least it meant one less vehicle to clog up the roads.

What made me change my mind, paradoxically, was realising just how much of the British countryside I had missed by having no vehicle of my own. It was a trip to see the ospreys nesting on Speyside that nailed the point home most forcibly.

I had journeyed up (with conscience intact) on a sleeper from Euston, and for no extra charge had been able to watch throngs of grouse and red deer through the dawn mists. One of the advantages, as I shall elaborate later, of watching from a moving hide!

I got off the train at Aviemore with ten miles still to go to the eyrie at Loch Garten, and less than twelve hours before I was due back in Edinburgh for a business appointment. There was little choice but to take a taxi. But I didn't feel it was right to be ferried to the threshold so I asked the driver to drop me off on the edge of Abernethy Forest, which he did with remarkable nonchalance, considering it was half-past-five on a drizzly April morning.

But I was glad I did walk that last stretch. I saw more in one hour on those deserted Highland lanes than I did the whole of the rest of the day. There were roe deer and red squirrels edging through the forest, crossbills swinging in the pine-tops, and capercaillies as big as turkeys blustering in the middle of the road.

It's probably true that I would have seen little of this if I'd stayed in the taxi. But just as true that the trip would have been impossible without a car of some sort, given the time I had available. Unless you have the time to be a professional cyclist or rambler, many of the most exciting wildernesses in Britain are, for all practical purposes, inaccessible if you are not a car owner. It is one of the many ironies associated with motoring that it can give you the chance to be *more* natural. You can take off, when and where you wish, without any elaborate planning. Even if you live in the heart of a city, you can wake on an April morning and be amongst the primroses within an hour. I would judge this to be the one ecological virtue of the motor car: that provided a man can bring himself to step out of it, it can put him back in his natural habitat when the mood takes him.

So much for the defence. Against it is a formidable charge list of pillage, murder and poisoning. It begins, not with the car itself, but with the insatiable demands for new territory that it makes.

The new road

There are something like 5,000 acres of countryside swallowed up by roadbuilding operations each year, but the actual area may be less important than the character of what is lost. Ponds may have to be drained. Woods can be chopped in two, creating dangerous crossing situations for their bird and animal inhabitants. Plant colonies which depend for their development on the gradual edging forward of their roots may be stopped in their tracks by the tarmac.

But the impact of a new road is not wholly against the interests of the area's wildlife. Where the road is dug out through a cutting for instance, it can expose a new soil surface and bring new plant communities in its wake. When Bulford Camp on Salisbury Plain was excavated for a new road in 1939, dormant seeds of that beautiful scarlet buttercup, pheasant's eye, were brought to the surface, and flowered in their thousands in the chalk rubble at the side of the road.

Something similar happened more recently in Wiltshire. During the building of the M4 a number of old chalky fields were bulldozed over. A number of the traditional arable weeds, which are cleaned out of contemporary crop-seed, flowered later that year as a result. Blue pimpernel, venus's looking-glass and small toadflax had been seen near this site many years before. But night-scented catchfly, pheasant's eye and pawnbroker's plant (so called from its cluster of three seeds) were new.

On both occasions the pheasant's eyes, being annuals, were short-lived delights: they vanished as soon as the verges had been grassed over. But more permanent plant communities can develop along new roads and play a vital role in the survival of creatures like butterflies.

Many species of butterfly are being pressed into dwindling countryside ghettoes as development and new farming practices destroy their caterpillars' food plants. Chalk – loving species are especially vulnerable. Butterflies like blues, clinging onto vestigial and isolated patches of downland, stand little chance if they're suddenly ploughed up for kale, or if heavy-footed cattle replace sheep as the grazing animals. Even if this change happens when the butterflies are on the wing they will be lucky if they can find a nearby patch of the right plants on which to lay their eggs.

But new road verges, linked as they are with the whole road system, form part of a linear habitat of enormous length. Verge management programmes are beginning to take account of the needs of wild flowers and insects. Even if there is a change of management, and a strip of verge is mown when a food plant is full-grown, or bulldozed up for a new gas-pipe, there's every hope that flying butterflies at least will migrate along the verge to the nearest undisturbed stretch. There is evidence that blues have actually increased along the M1, as its verges are colonised by clovers and trefoils.

Chalk is stable at almost any incline, and doesn't need the covering of alien soil that is sometimes spread over it. This new embankment in Wiltshire has been colonised to this extent in one year.

Even the devastation that inevitably accompanies the building of a new road can provide temporary accommodation for more adaptable plants and animals. The rough ground along the road edges that has been churned up by the bulldozers is rapidly colonised by fast-growing opportunist weeds like groundsel, shepherd's purse and fat hen.

Even birds can sometimes find a home amongst the rubble. I remember one summer when a colony of sand-martins cashed-in on a temporary sandbank raised during the building of a new roundabout in Middlesex. This is how I described them at the time:

> The contractors were building a roundabout on a busy arterial road that ran up a hill covered with a light gravelly soil. They had cut into the hill and exposed a vertical face about 20 yards long and 10 feet high. This operation, I suppose, was complete in February. By mid-April, about a dozen of these sleek brown birds, one of the very first visitors to arrive in this country from Africa, were starting to excavate their 2ft deep nesting tunnels. To them, this bank, about as secure as a sand-castle on a beach, was as good accommodation as the dry cliffs that are their natural habitat. Towards the end of June I would watch the parent birds ferrying food to the young, from my Green Line bus which passed within yards of the bank. Then one evening in July, the young were out, flickering like ticker-tape above the traffic jam. Two weeks later the bank was levelled off and planted with grass. I never found out whether this timing was an act of kind-heartedness by the builders or just a happy accident. It seemed a small miracle whichever it was, this home for a season in a substance that is a symbol for change and insecurity.
>
> from Richard Mabey, *The Unofficial Countryside* (1973)

Along minor roadworks these temporary delights and the relatively quick healing of the scars perhaps make up for the disturbance and loss of habitat. But a major piece of roadbuilding is another matter. A new motorway destroys so much countryside and is such a permanent and conspicuous feature of the landscape that the way it fits into its natural surroundings can't be ignored. Nature can rapidly smooth over the minor blemishes man inflicts on the landscape; but it can't easily seal a hill which has been gashed through the middle or hide two hundred feet of raised tarmac. In these situations it is vital that the roadbuilders take positive action to repair the damage they have done.

In 1956, the then Ministry of Transport set up the Landscape Advisory Committee composed of professional architects, foresters, representatives of amenity groups and motoring organisations. In theory, its function is twofold: to advise on the routing of all new major roads, including motorways, and to recommend design and landscaping features that will help these roads blend as 'naturally' as possible with the surrounding countryside. In practice, the first of these aims is little more than a gesture towards the notion of public participation. Almost without exception it's the road engineers who have the final say about the route a road should take. On too many occasions the Government has shown its contempt for the views of its advisory committee and the public at large in favour of the dogmatic decisions of its engineers and penny-pinching economists. Hundreds of acres of ancient downland have been wiped out, Nature Reserves cut in half and Areas of Outstanding Natural Beauty desecrated.

But once a route has been fixed, the committee's advice about how to minimise its damaging effects on the landscape is taken much more seriously.

The policy which underpins the landscaping of new motorways and trunk roads is that they must be made to blend with the surrounding country as much as possible.* This is as much for the benefit of the motorists using the road as for those who live and work in its vicinity. Many of the practical measures taken to achieve this end are beyond the scope of this book. There is the design of bridges to be considered, the radius of curves round the edge of a hill, the exposure of attractive rock strata.

*If, however, planting is ever done for contrast, not harmony, it must be on a grand scale, like the rows of huge Lombardy poplars that range across the French plains.

The landscaping and safety requirements on motorways can produce wide expanses of grassland, as on this stretch of the M1 near Hemel Hempstead.

One of the chief ways in which the new road can be made to 'bleed' into the adjacent country is by imaginative planning of the verges. This means planting with native and local tree species where the surrounding landscape is wooded (in 1967 nearly a million new trees were planted along motorways and trunk roads), but also knowing when *not* to plant, as the Landscape Advisor to the Ministry of Transport pointed out in 1969:

> On the downs it may be a case of *not* planting . . . but of shaping the earthworks to merge as smoothly as possible into the flowing contours. Here of course the alignment must be faultless. Ideally the only planting needed might be a clump or two of beech in a stategic position, almost certainly off the road where we do not own the land and cannot plant. To be realistic, though, some scars are unavoidable and if they are conspicuous they will need to be masked by planting. . . .

Basically what we are still trying to do in each case is to bring the countryside, of whatever type, right up to the road, as in the case of minor roads. Because we are viewing it at speed, however, the planting must be on a grander scale, still linking with the local planting pattern, framing the views, healing any unavoidable scars, but always bold enough for any desired effect to last long enough to make its impact – groups of trees rather than single specimens, larger gaps through which a view is seen, contrast in the texture of grass arising from varied maintenance techniques rather than the interest of groups of wild flowers.

from M. R. Porter, 'Road Verges and Landscape'
in *Road Verges. Their Function and Management*

This point about 'viewing at speed' is crucial to motorway planting. Whereas a pedestrian travels about twenty-two feet in five seconds, a driver on a motorway may cover a quarter of a mile. At 60mph he is viewing, in one minute, one solid mile of planting. It is only possible at this speed to give a precis of the

An example of the extensive planting carried out by the Department of the Environment along motorways; the M1 near Kegworth in Leicestershire

landscape. This is why there is neither use nor place along rural motorways for single, small trees, or pruned exotics that would stick out as awkwardly as lamp standards. It is well-shaped and sensitively positioned clumps of native trees that will both please the traveller and help temper the hard edge of the road that are needed – oaks and beech in pasture land, ash in limestone country, pine, birch and rowan in the uplands.

But there is a place for low-lying plants as well. On moorland, where a neat grass verge would look ludicrous, the heather and bracken can be allowed to spread naturally to the edge of the hard shoulder. Broom, with its showers of brilliant chrome yellow flowers, is ideal for sandy embankments. And as I've described in the next section, the areas of hydro-sown grass along the verges, something like 13·7 acres per mile, quickly develop their own natural flora. Some species, like the wild daffodils which have established themselves along the Ross spur on the M50, can put on as spectacular a show for the traveller as the bulkier shrubs and trees.

But even the most inconspicuous plants aren't redundant on motorway verges. Because these strips of grass are inaccessible to pickers, are rarely nagged by excavation for new sewers and gas pipes, and – once established – are only infrequently mown under a strict regime laid down by the Department of the Environment, wild flowers can build up quite large colonies along them. From here they can spread into the adjacent countryside. A mature motorway verge becomes, in effect, a wild nursery, an area from which plants can repopulate those natural habitats in which they're increasingly harassed.

Hitch-hikers

As well as the plants that are actively planted and encouraged along trunk roads, there are others that flourish precisely because of the conditions created by motor traffic. Two, in particular, have gone so far as to make use of the modern pneumatic tyre as a vehicle for ferrying their seeds about!

The timeless magic of the English country lane

Not even the most fertile motorway can really match these ancient and intimate trackways; and no amount of manicuring restore their character once they've been 'improved':

. . . to widen and straighten a lane quite simply destroys it. A lane *is* its boundaries, its containing banks and walls and trees and hedges, its windings and unexpected corners: 'improvement' merely substitutes a new route in the old position, like pulling down an old building to put up a new one. And for many country-lovers old lanes are far greater treasures than old buildings. They are our closest experience of the country, an intricate net of ways through the very substance of the countryside, more intimately delightful than anything now left in our landscape, and for birds and animals green ribbons of refuge in open farmland.

from Nan Fairbrother, *New Lives, New Landscapes* (1970)

The spiky-leaved North American rush *juncus tenuis* was not known in this country before 1883, but in the sixty years that followed it had spread into fifty British counties, most abundantly along the edges of roads and tracks. A close look at the seeds of this rush can give a clue as to how this happened. They're very small (it takes 10,000 to cover a square inch) and shaped like a minute baby's feeding bottle. When they get wet, they become slimy and slightly sticky, and are easily picked up by passing tyres.

But once a route has been fixed, the committee's advice about pineapple weed from the fruity perfume given off when you walk over it – that has given the most conclusive evidence of the hitch-hiking of seeds. This is now one of our commonest flowers, well known not just for the smell of its leaves but for its yellow button blossoms, like daisies without the petals. Those who are familiar with the plant will know how closely it follows the edges of tracks and parking places. Before 1900 pineapple weed was rare in this country, yet in the next twenty-five years it had spread over the whole of England. These were the years during which regular motor traffic was becoming established, and also the time when many roads were still a sea of mud for much of the year. It's likely that, as with the North American rush, the nature of pineapple weed's fruits had a good deal to do with its spread – they have ribbed treads that grip like a radial tyre. But then again, without the muddy condition of the roads it's likely that this spread would have been much slower. Mud containing the seeds was no doubt picked up by the tyres and carried quite long distances before it dried out and flaked off. Rain would then sluice the seeds – ready pelleted by a fine silt – to the road's edge where, with luck, they would take root.

For those who are sceptical about the possibility of a fast-moving saloon picking up such delicate freight, let me recount an experiment that was carried out in the Midlands in 1968. A car with scrupulously scrubbed tyres was driven along sixty-five miles of road after a period of heavy rain. On the way it was turned periodically into passing places, field gateways and so on. At the end of the journey the tyres were hosed down, and the sediment collected from the washings. This was incubated in sterilised compost and in a few months had produced thirteen different species of flowering plant, including 220 seedlings of pineapple weed. In the light of figures like that it's fascinating to imagine what the future of this plant would have been without the motorcar.

Coriander

This North African spice plant is one of the odd species that has sprung up unassisted along the verges of the M1 in the ten years since it was opened. It would probably be true, for once, to say that it fell off the back of a lorry.

It was discovered during a thorough survey of the motorway's flora carried out in the summer of 1970 under the joint sponsorship of the Nature Conservancy and the Ministry of Transport. Teams of student botanists, dressed for safety's sake in orange fluorescent waistcoats and armed with Keble Martin's *Concise British Flora in Colour*, studied fifty-yard stretches of verge centred on the mile posts between Hendon and Leeds – 185 in all. As well as listing the plants present, they measured the width and slope of the verge, the drainage and acidity of the soil, adjoining land use and tested for the presence of lead residue.

The full results of the survey had not been correlated at the time of going to press, but the inventory of plants is encouraging enough by itself. Three hundred and eighty-four species were identified, including such comparatively scarce species as purging flax, creeping jenny, yellow vetchling, dark mullein and pepper saxifrage, as well as that alien stowaway, coriander. This total included fifty-four species of grass, which represents nearly a third of all the British species.

It's a remarkable list, considering the amount of exhaust pollution that is sprayed out over the motorway each day, and it seems that the hard shoulder acts as a kind of aseptic cordon between the traffic and the verge.

Rescue

For all the chaos they inevitably create, roadbuilders are not normally actively hostile to the countryside. If they're approached in time and aren't committed to any labour themselves, they'll nearly always co-operate with naturalists in rescuing threatened colonies of plants and mammals. There was a remarkable Noah's Ark operation done on a family of Hertfordshire badgers at Bishops

Stortford on the route of the new M11. They were successfully transplanted 50 miles away to another disused sett.

And some rare plants have been almost literally snatched out of the jaws of the excavators. In 1971, a naturalised colony of lovage – one-time indigestion remedy, soup thickener and love charm – was found growing wild on a patch of waste ground at Hunslet, Leeds. Sadly the site of this rare relic of the medieval herb garden was only sixty-five yards from the advancing path of a new motorway into Leeds, and a tipping contractor soon buried it under bricks and concrete rubble. But the lovage had friends in high places.

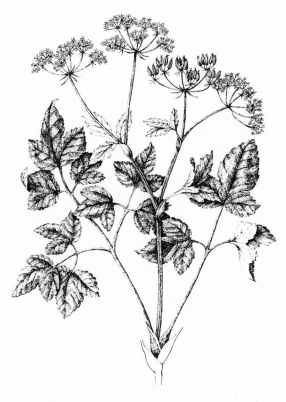

Lovage

The botanists who discovered it were students of Dr G. A. Nelson, one-time president of the Leeds Naturalists' Club. He went to the corporation and secured a promise that the rubble would be removed from the lovage. It was, and though the plant had been buried for ten days, it survived.

The same year a colony of wild columbine was destroyed in Nottinghamshire during the work on the extension of the M1. It would have been tragic if these flowers had been lost completely, for columbine is one of the rarest and most beautiful of our native flowers. But luckily members of the county naturalists' trust had had the foresight to take action before the bulldozers arrived.

John Clare described the colour of wild columbine as 'stone-blew or deep night-brown'.

They collected the seeds of these doomed plants and, with some poetic justice I feel, obtained permission to plant eighty-odd seedlings in the grounds of a maintenance depot on the motorway. Later in the year motorway staff transferred the plants to the newly constructed motorway verges, as close to the original site as possible. There is a nice echo of old herbal magic in the story of these enterprising Nottinghamshire naturalists: columbine is named after the dove but was believed to be the food of lions. Rub some on your hands and it built your courage up!

These were exceptional rescues and rare plants, though pointers to what can be done with a little foresight and perseverance. But perhaps the most practical example, and one which any lively school biology class would be especially fitted to follow, is the continuing transplanting of primroses by the South Hams Society in Devon.

The steep-banked lanes in Devon have always been renowned for their primroses, but holiday traffic has been increasing so much in this part of the world that even minor roads are being widened. Often this means the removal of the banks and their replacement by fences, but where the road goes through a cutting there will at least be a bare bank left which is more or less equivalent to the original hedgebank. It's these virgin cuttings which the South Hams amenity group has been recolonising with primroses.

The procedure they follow is not complicated, and can serve perfectly well as a model for other parts of the country and, for that matter, for other types of wild flower. All that's needed is a supply of plants, some willing helpers to bed them out, and the blessing of the Highways Authority. It would be a exceptionally churlish authority that would withhold this – in Devon they have gone as far as to lend a water-cart to the volunteers so that the primroses can be watered as soon as they are planted.

The original source of the Devon primroses was a hillside that was due to be ploughed up. Other sources have included steep corners of private woods and old orchards. If advance information about road-widening schemes can be obtained – constant scrutiny of the plans for projected roads is crucial for any plant rescue –

it might be possible to obtain permission to take the plants from the old embankment and replant them on the new. But remember that digging up roadside plants without permission is illegal in most counties, and transplanting from *unthreatened* verges would simply defeat the purpose of the exercise.

In Devon the primroses are dug up with trowels – keeping as much of the long root as possible – and transplanted in open trugs and flat wicker baskets. When they reach their new home a deep hole is dug for each plant, so that the roots can reach down into the moist soil below the surface. They're planted more thickly at the top of the banks, as they take better in the richer and undisturbed topsoil here. The plants will in any case slowly colonise the lower slopes as humus builds up on the raw surface of the cuttings.

As the Devon planters point out, the job is by no means soft work, especially when you are working on a one in three gradient! But there is some compensation in the fact that the primroses can be transplanted whilst they are in full bloom and at their most fragrant.

Devon has preserved more than just primroses:

Primrose planters in Devon

The Roads Committee have been greatly assisted in their policy of wild flower conservation by local societies and by the co-operation of staffs and pupils of the schools controlled by the county's Education Committee. The latter have been kind enough to participate in a continuous scheme for the collection of wild flower seeds for dissemination on banks and road works where loss or damage of the indigenous vegetation might occur following excavation and the operation of heavy plant for road improvements. . . . The harvested seed (cleaned and prepared for use by the chairman of our Southern Area Roads Committee, his wife and other helpers) was incorporated in the mixture used for spray-seeding two of the appropriate sites.

County Surveyor of Devon, quoted in
The Settle and District Civic Society Report 1971

It's evidence again of just what can be achieved by keeping a constantly vigilant eye on the activities of the developers, being prepared to approach the authorities with constructive suggestions, *and* helping with the work yourself.

But one slight word of caution to anyone who is now raring to scatter seeds over every vacant roadside lot. Do confine yourself to the commonest wild flowers that bloom naturally in such places. Cow parsley, poppies, buttercups, ox-eye daisies are ideal, having seeds which are easy to gather and making a fine show when they're in full bloom. Don't add to the problems of nearby farmers by sowing 'weed' seeds.* They'll find their own way there soon enough. Above all, don't gather or sow the seeds of any scarce plants, or species which don't occur naturally in your area. If you are in any doubt, consult your local naturalists' trust.

It would not take many packets of over-enthusiastically scattered nurseryman's variegated columbines to start playing havoc with the wild stock – and certainly with the records of those botanists who have been painstakingly trying to map the·changing fortunes of our wild flowers.

*The Weeds Act of 1959 defines the following as 'injurious weeds': spear thistle, creeping thistle, curled dock, broad-leaved dock, ragwort.

Roadside reserves

One of the happier side-effects of road construction is the creation of little pockets of land that are too oddly shaped or too close to fast-moving traffic to be put to any economic use. Because of the danger they're not troubled much by human visitors either, and often develop into miniature sanctuaries for wildlife. (They're often known as 'reserves'.) Those little copses cut off like islands when a road forks temporarily into a dual carriageway are especially good. So are roundabouts, provided they are not too fastidiously landscaped.

There are too the strips of grassland that run down the central reservations of dual carriageways. These are a favourite site for inky cap fungi (close cousins of *coprinus atramentarius*, p 30) that come up like shaggy white busbies, then quickly dissolve into a thick black juice. Their attachment to these reservations is in part due to the household refuse that is often used to bulk up the foundation soil on new roads. Inky caps are coprophilous fungi – they live off dead organic matter – and they prosper on a combination of underground food and well-mown turf to grow above. Incidentally, if you can find some that aren't inside a thoroughly impregnable reservation and haven't yet started to 'melt', pick a few and fry them. They're one of the best edible wild fungi. If they have started to dissolve – try utilising the black juice as a marking ink like they did in the fifteenth century.

Bank voles can also flourish on the more densely vegetated of these reservations, undisturbed as they are by humans and other land-based predators. They seem to have a preference for the motorway verges and are probably the chief reason why kestrels have

Bank vole

become such a regular and distracting feature of modern motorways. There can be few travellers who haven't noticed these elegant little falcons hovering above the traffic, flickering and holding against the wind in a perfectly controlled stall. It is a mystery what they are looking for sometimes, arched out over the centre of the carriageway – until you realise what prodigious eyesight they have. At fifty feet above ground level, a kestrel is capable of spotting – and eventually grabbing – prey over a hundred feet from the point above which it's poised.

There is a theory that it's not just the abundance of voles in these undisturbed verge sanctuaries that have made them so attractive to kestrels. Those falcons may have joined the trend to convenience foods. A number of experiments have shown that vibrations from heavy vehicles tend to drive earthworms and beetles, on which kestrels occasionally feed, to the surface, making them easy picking for insectivorous birds like rooks. It may be that small mammals also tend to stay on the surface more when the ground is being vibrated. But this is only a theory at present.

We are likely to know more about motorway kestrels when the survey which the Young Ornithologists' Club organised during the summer of 1973 is published. This junior branch of the Royal Society for the Protection of Birds asked its members to look out for hovering kestrels as they were driven along the motorways during their summer holidays. The exact position of the kestrels was noted by reference to the motorway junction numbers.

This is a survey which other groups of young people could well follow up, particularly if they could carry it out over two or three years. Some idea of whether the number of kestrels in evidence is related to time of day, increased traffic density, etc, might throw up some valuable clues about this fascinating adaptation.

There is a chance that kestrels will become the first bird species to adapt completely to the motorway as a habitat. Nest boxes are being erected along some motorways in the hope that the birds may be tempted to breed as well as hunt there.

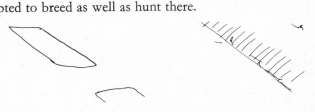

The roundabout in the approach to the shopping centre in Hemel Hempstead New Town carries a stream in a deep gulley through its centre, which is brightened by wild marsh marigolds in spring.

The village green in Monks Eleigh, Suffolk, a fine site for grassland flowers

This small pond, formed in a roadside hollow in Buckinghamshire, is a regular feeding ground for swallows and house martins in the summer.

And reserves for humans too! Although this island at the junction of two lanes in North Norfolk is over a mile from the nearest village, some benefactor provided it with a seat. From it you can watch bramblings fielding in the fields in the winter, and sand martins nesting in a disused quarry nearby.

Cars as Hides

The real point of a nature reserve is more to protect the wildlife than amuse the visitors. It's hardly fair to expect accidental roadside sanctuaries to be treated in this way, but the principles are the same: wild creatures and humans do not mix easily, and if the function of the reserve is to be fulfilled without banishing the sightseers altogether, it's vital that the two are separated.

It may come as a surprise that the car, slaughterer and wreaker of devastation, is as good a barrier as any in this respect – at least from the occupant's point of view. Birds probably have a marginal preference for thatched marshland hides that don't mow them down, but even so are astonishingly tolerant of motor vehicles. Anything to cover up the scent and sight of Man, still hated and feared in the flesh more than any of his technological artefacts. So fixed are birds in this fear that they will perch unconcerned only feet away from the blur of lethally fast moving traffic, yet keep a safe distance from parked cars with those predatory silhouettes visible inside.

For all that, there's no more convenient or comfortable place from which to watch birds. I was heading homewards in a car when I saw my first red-backed shrike, perched contemptuously on the very top of one of the roadside hawthorns where I had searched for it on foot all afternoon. And I got my best view of a hobby in the same way, only on this occasion the car was moving and I was not. I was coasting at walking speed along a heathland lane in East Suffolk, when this sickle-winged falcon glided so low over the car that I tumbled out of it without putting on the brake.

Hide – and bird-table too. In frost or deep snow you can park your car at the edge of a wood, sprinkle nuts and seed on the bonnet and sit and wait for the show to begin on the other side of the windscreen. You will need to be patient and keep perfectly still, but if you can you stand a chance of seeing more exciting birds at closer quarters than you ever would at a garden feeder. Not only the usual tits and greenfinches have been known to come and feed on car bonnets in these conditions, but nuthatches, woodpeckers, and even hawfinches.

I was going to add as a further advantage your own cosiness and

Eric Hosking's famous driver's-seat snap of a Houbara bustard. This bird from the deserts of the Middle East somehow found its way to a frost-riven Suffolk mustard field in the winter of 1962. It was the first bird of this species to visit Britain for over sixty years, and so numerous and noisy were the sightseers (they were even arriving in charabancs) that it became too nervous to photograph. Eric Hosking had virtually given up hope when he met it obligingly walking down the road towards his car.

relative protection from the arduous conditions being suffered by the birds. But that I think must be counted as one of the black marks against car-watching. I still remember with some shame the day I spent watching the spring wader migration in north Norfolk from inside a comfortable saloon, keeping the visibility up with the windscreen wipers. Insulating yourself out of sheer laziness from the rigours of the outdoors is not the way to get to grips with wild creatures. You miss so much: some sympathy with the way the animals have to cope with climate and environment; the more subtle and imperceptible changes in soil and plants and their resident creatures that you can only appreciate on foot. Bird song can be drowned by the engine noise and the smell of the flowers completely masked. And unless you are in the passenger's seat, trying to identify that tantalising orchid at speed is likely to add you to the ditch compost.

So using your car as a hide is a mixed business, as likely to cut you off from your prey as to help you watch it more closely. Its delights and frustrations have never been better described than by the motoring writer H. F. Ellis:

Birds are deceptive at speed – at the observer's speed, that is. I have known the wing-bars of a chaffinch flash so brightly against a hedgerow at sixty miles an hour as to suggest that a woodchat shrike was making an unexpected call. Yellow-hammers are unmistakable at any speed, and so are the white rumps of bullfinches. But linnets get curiously elongated; and whitethroats, unless they are conveniently fluttering up and down in that nuptial way they have, may look full of exotic promise. Ducks in flight are terrible and add to a passenger's difficulties by always heading in the opposite direction. No duck has ever flown alongside a car in the whole history of birdwatching. Even seagulls are only now learning that many motorists leave handsome trails of discarded food behind them.

So, for the motoring birdman in a passenger role, there is much frustration, many a putative merlin gone with the wind, a long list of possible ospreys half-glimpsed over lochs, of wood sandpipers all but declaring themselves at disappearing sewage farms; fallings from us, vanishings – as Wordsworth, who never raised more than a jog-trot in his life, so imaginatively put it . . .

The man in command of his vehicle, and preferably alone, is in an altogether different case. Here the car, stoppable at will, comes into its own as a commodious portable hide. It is particularly good for buzzards, who will remain unmoved on their telegraph poles while you roll gently to a halt a bare twenty yards away. I have got closer to predators of all kinds by car – owls, harriers, shrikes, even a peregrine falcon posed majestically on the scooped-out face of a small quarry in north Cornwall – than I have even been able to achieve on foot. E. W. Hendy, who wrote so well about Somerset birds (and incidentally put all hoopoe-on-the-lawn people in their places for ever by spotting a woodcock on his, not to mention a cream-coloured courser on the golf links at Minehead), used his car for blackcock.

> Heath poults, to use the local name for black grouse, are wary birds and near approach to them is usually difficult. But when the blackcock are engaged in their nuptial display it is easy to obtain a good view of this curious performance by means of motor-car, provided that the 'lekking' place is so situated that a car can be driven near to it.

He knew of such a place on Exmoor and would drive there early on a May morning, to watch the pantomime at ease in his 'motor-car'.

At least, I hope he was at ease. It has to be admitted that observation from a car, even a stationary car, is not always free from care. The perfect ornithological saloon has yet to be produced by the manufacturers. There are obstructions. Windows mist up. The best view is often to be had from the back when one is in front, and *vice-versa*. I have known the gear-lever to go clean up my trouser-leg, when I was crouching down to rest my binoculars on the window-ledge. And the amount of movement an observed bird will tolerate inside this outwardly harmless carapace is strictly limited. Windows must be lowered with infinite caution. The raising of binoculars can be fatal. Certainly no bird within forty feet will watch unmoved the jack-knifing of some ponderous rump *en-route* from front seat to back. It is better, if the move must be made, to slip out of the farther door and creep, doubled-up under cover of the car, into the back – though the performance, if another car happens to pass, may look as curious as lekking. What is urgently required is a driver's seat that can be swivelled imperceptibly round through 360 degrees, as provided in the better kind of Pullman coach.

It would be folly to suggest that most or even much bird-watching is better done from inside a car. Birds in flight are hidden instantly by the roof. All kinds of woodland and river-side birds, skulking birds, restless or reedy birds – these must be sought out in their habitats and there be sat down and waited for. Nor do we want mudflats and reservoirs, reed-beds and cliff tops to be lined with cars full of nature lovers, however cautiously they may lower their windows. The territory I have in mind for car watching is open country: wide plains and moorland, and bare mountain roads, where the only cover of any kind, short of lying in a bog or curling up with adders in the heather, is the inside of your 1100 De Luxe. Predator country. Predators keep still (even in the air, some of them) and sit proud on posts. Their contempt for cars is wholesome and complete. They are in all ways incomparable.

from H. F. Ellis, 'Ornithological Saloons',
in *The Countryman* (autumn 1969)

Tailpiece
We were leaving the Etchingham station car park in Sussex on a very hot day when we were astounded to see a lizard clinging to the number plate of the Mercedes-Benz car in front. We followed

for about four miles and the lizard still clung on although he did move his long tail. We were not able to overtake the car to tell the driver. I can only think that the car had been parked all day with its rear close to a bank and that the lizard climbed aboard to sun himself on the hot bodywork.

Letter in The Countryman

The Night

Since your portable hide is effectively equipped with searchlights, it's an ideal place to watch wildlife from at night. Most of our mammal species prefer to move about and feed in the dark, and your best chance of catching a glimpse of a fox, badger or deer is when it is lit up in a car's headlamp beam.

It's not absolutely clear why the majority of our mammals should be largely nocturnal whilst, for instance, most of our bird species go about their business by day. There are of course advan-

Fox

tages in working a kind of night shift. You can exploit food sources which are used by other creatures during the day, but without having to obtain them in direct competition. So hedgehogs hunt down perambulating slugs, also largely nocturnal, at night, whilst thrushes root them out from their hiding places during the day.

But there can be little survival value any more in the protective cover of darkness. Although this may have been the origin of nocturnal adaptations, there are now just as many predators adapted to hunting in the dark as there are prey species. During the day a bank vole may only have hovering kestrels to keep a look-out for. But once night has fallen there will be badgers, foxes and any number of owls.

Barn owls, incidentally, may have learned to make use of vehicles during their night-time hunting sorties. There have been too many reports of them crossing and recrossing lanes in front of cars over quite long distances for this to be purely coincidence. The barn owls clearly aren't interested in the light from the headlamps; even with their backs to the car, they probably find some difficulty in focussing down enough to avoid being dazzled. It's more likely that, like wagtails following grazing cattle, they are relying on the noise and disturbance created by the car to stir small animals on the verge into movement.

Sadly, many of these barn owls do not survive long enough to collect their meals. I have discussed animal road accidents at length later in the book, but it cannot be said too often that animals and birds whose eyes are adapted to hunting in the dark are very easily blinded by car headlights and are unable to take evasive action. If you come across an animal in the road at night, slow down and dim your headlights as much as safety will allow until it has escaped.

One type of slaughter that even the safest driver cannot avoid is that of night-flying insects and moths, which hunt nectar in those flowers that stay open during darkness. If you are interested in studying dead specimens (I must confess I am not) you could look on your car as a rough and ready trap. The insects' carcasses will be somewhat mangled, but at least they will save you killing fresh specimens.

Human pressure

But the chief impact of new roads on the ecology of a locality is due not so much to the sheer physical disturbance of the land that precedes them, as to the vast numbers of new humans introduced into the landscape in their wake. Some of the effects are permanent and go away beyond the boundaries of the road. Once there is road access, new towns and airports can spring up, swallowing up incomparably larger areas of countryside than were ever lost under the road itself. Small farms close down as men leave them to work in new industrial estates. Even the perception of time – still measured in the countryside by the span of daylight and the movement of the seasons – can change. Old villages, which have suddenly become within an hour's drive of a city centre, are transformed into commuter dormitories. In a district which has had a new major road struck through it, the pattern of life on the land – wild and well as human – can never be entirely the same again.

But it is probably the pressure of *leisure* motoring which has the biggest impact on the roadside environment itself. There have been a wide range of studies on this problem, and I would refer readers again to Allan Patmore's *Land and Leisure* for a full discussion. Let me just quote a few figures to give some idea of the scale of the assault which roadside wildlife has to put up with.

In 1973 there were more than 12,000,000 private cars on the road. A survey by the British Tourist Authority showed that 90 per cent of the users of these cars indulge in 'leisure' motoring at some time. Driving itself, in fact, is now the dominant outdoor leisure activity in most of the Western world and in any three-month period somewhere between 30 and 40 per cent of the population have taken a car 'trip' to the countryside. Rural car parks themselves are paradoxically the most popular objective, closely followed by any site with multiple attractions: a view, lavatories, picnic-tables and so on. A survey in Ashdown Forest, Sussex, showed that at this sort of site the minimum comfortable space needed by each car was 620 square feet; and although car-owners are twice as likely as non-owners to participate in other outdoor sports like golf, swimming and even walking, normally about 80 per cent of leisure motorists, having arrived in the country, either stay in their cars or picnic within six yards of them.

These figures, more than anything else, confirm both the importance and the vulnerability of roadside habitats. They are the natural surroundings with which we have the closest physical contact; equally, they are the most hard-pressed.

Fire

Car-borne tourists, smoking, picnicking, and cooking on their portable primuses, inevitably bring fire in their wake. Some of the areas most popular with the public – like the edges of conifer forests and furzy commons – are also the most dangerously inflammable. Hence those dramatic Forestry Commission fire hazard warning boards. In the dry heaths along the East Suffolk coastal strip there are on average 100 fires every year and 230 acres of heath burnt down as a result.

On this sort of country fires are a mixed blessing. Now that furze is no longer regularly cut for cottage hearths and bakers' ovens, heaths would soon develop into scrub and woodland if it weren't for the occasional burn-off. And there are certain flowers, like rose-bay willow-herb, that flourish in burnt areas because of the increased nitrates in the soil. But the sort of indiscriminate and uncontrolled burning that is the end-product of a carelessly dropped match does considerably more harm than good. Most of these fires occur in the summer months, when the heath vegetation is parched dry and the tourist population at its densest. The conse-

quences for scarce heathland nesters like nightjars and stonechats can be disastrous.

The photo above was taken on one such heath in north Norfolk, after an Easter Bank Holiday fire which burnt out about three acres. As bad luck would have it, the area was a dense gorse thicket which sheltered a nesting colony of something like thirty pairs of shelduck. I discovered the scorched nest mounds a few days after the fire. Many of the eggs had been baked solid in their shells. Nearer the edge of the fire they'd been no more than blackened, but the flames had been enough to make the ducks desert, and crows and rats had moved in to suck out this bountiful and unexpected food source. No wonder: there were up to a dozen eggs in each nest, each one as big as a chicken's.

Incidentally, when shelducks do hatch successfully, they can provide one of the most endearing wildlife spectacles to be met on the road. When the chicks are about eight weeks old they leave the nest, and are led by the parent birds in procession down to the nearest open water, usually a coastal mud-flat. Normally the female leads the crocodile and the male follows along behind. When they have to cross a road they marshal their brood as efficiently as school-crossing patrollers.

All open country – especially light sandy soil where parking and turning aren't obstructed by trees or man-made obstacles – is vulnerable to erosion. Like successive waves of pioneering frontiersmen, motorists driving off the road will move up to the edge of the territory opened up by their predecessors, and advance its boundary by a few inches.

On Ivinghoe Beacon in Buckinghamshire the constant flow of sightseers has worn the turf on the car park and main footpath down to the bare chalk. A swathe nearly ten feet wide in places has been shorn not just of its ground flora – a delightful mixture of chalk-loving orchids, eyebrights and gentians – but also of its topsoil. The owners, the National Trust, have decided to close this area for a number of years and replace the soil in the hope that the turf will become re-established.

Kelling Heath, only a few miles away from the burnt-out shelduck colony, is being literally worn away by tourist traffic.

But pounding by tyres and feet doesn't always erode the ground flora completely. In areas where the soil is heavy and human pressure light, plants which grow in flat rosettes like daisies and plantains are able to flourish. Their leaves, growing flush with the ground, are much less damaged by the traffic which passes over them than those of taller plants.

And as a final indication of how even apparently trivial human pressures can influence plant growth, have a look at the vegetation round the litter bins and benches in rural parking places. You'll often find a lush growth of coarse grass and weeds quite unlike the ground flora of the surrounding area. Near bins this is a result of the nutrients washed down from sandwich scraps and old newspaper. In places where humans are apt to sit awhile to enjoy the view, these unofficial fertilisers are supplemented by phosphates from cigarette ends!

Erosion only becomes a problem when vehicles are moving over a site regularly and in large numbers, so it's just as much a product of the popularity and accessibility of a spot, how parking is controlled, and the general traffic density in the area, as of the nature of the soil and type of vehicles crossing it. It consequently becomes part of the overall problem of how to control the motorcar in the countryside, which I will be looking at briefly in the final section of this book.

Animal accidents

Two problems which are more general along roads are animal road accidents and pollution.

There's no denying that deer can be a nuisance. Their sheer size doesn't help. A pair of rutting stags once completely blocked the A35 for three hours. The white deer below took a heavy toll of the vegetables in nearby gardens. Yet though a glimpse of a white stag with antlers locked in the moonlight might be a rare treat for

A pure white fallow deer killed by a car in the National Trust's park at Ashridge. He was a legendary beast, this nine-year-old buck, notorious for his raids on local gardens and allotments. A friend of mine whose house backs onto the park was woken one autumn night to find him jousting with another stag on his lawn.

a privileged few, I can't believe that the rest regard our most beautiful mammals as pests because of their occasional mischiefs. So the lack of care and respect shown to deer by most motorists is not easy to understand. In Ashridge Park, for instance, there are deer warning signs along all the major roads. Yet drivers still race along them at extraordinary speeds, and run down something like 10 per cent of the 200-strong herd every year.

Now the National Trust has taken more drastic measures to protect the animals. A series of concrete ramps has been built across the roads near the Estate's accident black-spots. Along many of the other roads, the scrub on the verges has been cut back to improve visibility for both deer and motorist.

The most promising accident-prevention technique so far introduced to the park was originally developed in the Netherlands. Polished steel mirrors mounted on top of posts about three feet high have been erected at the points where deer most often cross the roads. Most deer accidents occur at night, and the hope is that the mirrors will reflect car headlights and deter the animals from crossing when there is traffic about.

This system has been used in the Forest of Dean since the mid-sixties, and has reduced deer casualties there by about 10 per cent, but it does not work when reflected light is blocked out – by fog or thick snow for instance. And there was one sad occasion when a change in human social behaviour over-rode the beneficial effects of the mirrors. It occurred during the winter when British Summer Time was temporarily suspended. The effective 'putting forward' of the clock at this time meant that humans were forced to go about their business during the tail-end hours of darkness – to trespass into animals' time, in fact. During the murky mornings in January, a doe was killed nearly every morning by an early school bus passing through the forest.

The mirror system was introduced to Ashridge in 1972. The warden feels that it is a worthwhile exercise, in spite of these drawbacks:

We can't say this is going to be a 100 per cent guarantee

that deer won't cross when there is traffic about, but we hope it will do something to prevent the agonies deer suffer in road accidents. There is one deer now which I have got to shoot. It can't move its hind legs and it is a pitiful sight. It is not coming out during the day so I have not been able to shoot it yet. But I have seen it twice in my car headlights and I know it is suffering.

A survey by the British Trust for Ornithology during 1960–1 found 5,269 bird corpses on 341 miles of road, which suggests that over 2½ million birds are killed every year on British roads. The casualties on motorways, surprisingly, are much fewer, probably because there is such good visibility on them, and prospective crossers are often deterred by their breadth.

But it is no good becoming too sentimental about these enormous casualty figures. There are far more new animals and birds born every year than could ever be sustained by the food and territory available in our countryside. If some of the surplus were not killed by cars they would in all likelihood die of starvation or disease.

The trouble with the car is that it is an indiscriminate killer. It maims far more creatures than it ever despatches cleanly; it kills young and old, sick and fit alike. Unlike natural methods of population control, it doesn't confine itself to those animals that have surplus numbers. Those with a particular taste for roadside habitats or for feeding in the road, like owls, may actually be kept *below* their maximum populations in some areas by road accidents.

A number of local naturalists' societies keep annual records of casualties along selected stretches of road, and they can throw up some morbidly fascinating figures. In East Suffolk in 1966 and 1967 a count of corpses was made daily along roughly twenty miles of country road, following reports of abnormal casualties in the summer of 1966.

The very high mortality amongst mammals in 1966 (the 'other species' refer chiefly to hedgehogs and hares) at a time when bird deaths were normal suggests that perhaps a climatic factor was at work in this area, influencing the amount of plant food available

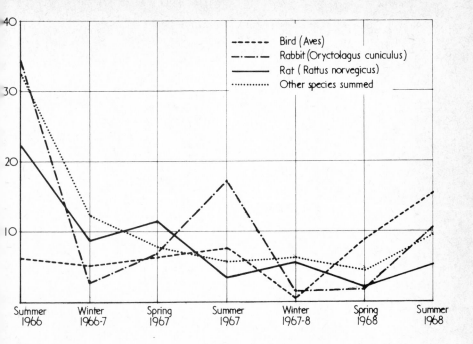

for the herbivores, and the general level of their population.

Yet bird casualties can be just as heavy. The following figures are those for corpses found on a five-mile stretch of the A47, a few miles to the north of the East Suffolk patch (see overleaf).

These figures show what a wide range of factors influence the numbers and species of the birds that are killed. Climate and the annual fluctuations in the abundance of various species clearly play a part. So does geography. That single year's crop of swallows may have been the result of a casual roadside nesting colony, and this corner of Norfolk is well-known for its barn owls.

But it is the birds' habits that are the over-riding factor. Although the very large number of moorhen fatalities is partly a result of the marshy character of this road, which runs parallel to the River Bure, it is the bird's habit of running across the road that is fatal for so many. Blackbirds suffer because they are low fliers; so are barn owls, which are doubly disadvantaged by the ease with

	1968	1969	1970	1971	Total
Lapwing	—	1	5	4	10
Rook	—	1	2	3	6
Swan	1	2	1	2	6
Skylark	2	—	—	3	5
Blackbird	8	—	3	2	13
Chaffinch	—	—	—	2	2
Redwing	—	—	—	2	2
Moorhen	32	39	62	46	179
Black-headed gull	6	13	26	31	76
House sparrow	11	6	4	15	36
Barn owl	4	1	6	1	12
Mallard	—	—	2	1	3
Fieldfare	—	—	1	1	2
Cuckoo	—	—	—	1	1
Herring gull	—	—	—	1	1
Swallow	5	—	—	—	5
Greenfinch	—	—	2	—	2
Greater black-backed gull	—	—	1	—	1
Starling	—	2	1	—	3
Red-throated diver	—	1	—	—	1

(Figures collected by members of the Norwich and Norfolk Naturalists' Society)

which their night-hunter's eyes are dazzled by headlights. House sparrows and black-headed gulls scavenge on the tarmac, and lapwings on the grass verges.

Understanding a little about what makes certain species particularly vulnerable can help us drive more cautiously and intelligently when there are animals about. Most nocturnal mammals and owls will stand a better chance of getting clear if you dip your lights. Birds like blackbirds which fly low and fast between hedgerows can usually be avoided if you take your foot briefly off the accelerator. And it's possible to predict, with something like 75 per cent accuracy, in which direction the road-surface feeding birds will fly off. If they're within three or four feet of one of the verges they will escape that way; if they're near the middle they will usually take off in the direction in which they are facing. If you are on a clear road it's neither difficult nor dangerous to steer a course based on these predictions.

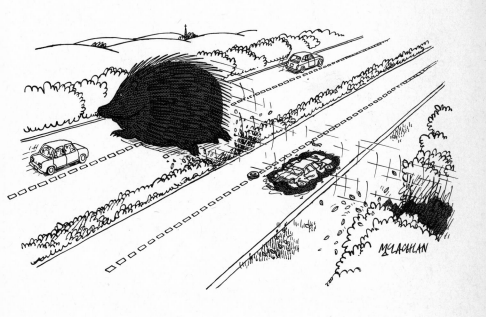

Some animals seem to be evolving their own evasive tactics. At one time a hedgehog caught in a car's headlights would just curl up and in all probability be run over. It was hardly a survival tactic which suited the situation, but it was the only one most hedgehogs knew. Now many naturalists have been observing a quite different reaction. Hedgehogs have been seen to stop in their tracks at the approach of a car, or to turn tail and run back onto the verge. It's not impossible that this is a genuine piece of evolution; that so many hedgehogs are being killed on the road that those non-conformists with a genetic tendency to flee rather than curl up at the approach of danger are surviving and increasing their strain.

Badgers are having less evolutionary luck. They still stick to their habit of turning manfully to face oncoming danger – motor cars included. Almost all badgers found dead on the road have been struck in the head or neck. The badger accident problem is exaggerated because, like toads, (p 76) they follow fixed tracks in their wanderings. When the Forestry Commission installed badger-flaps in many of their plantation fences they discovered that unless the gates were put directly in the path of the traditional tracks, they were simply ignored. No wonder then that if a new road is built across a badger track it doesn't instantly re-route the animal. So badgers continue to be slaughtered. In Somerset alone it's reckoned that over 1,000 are killed on the roads every year.

But there is hope for the badger. In Cheshire, on the M53, badgers have been provided with a man-made crossing, and by all accounts are using it. The motorway runs between two badger setts, but without cutting across a traditional track. So there was some chance of persuading the animals to use a crossing rather less intimidating than the open surface of the motorway. A special ledge was built along a culvert dug under the road to carry a valley brook, and a heavy net fence put up along one section of the road to deter the badgers from crossing above ground.

The idea is catching on. Already plans for badger underpasses are being discussed for the many motorways in Hertfordshire and for the M5 near Exeter.

Badgers and pedestrians yes, vehicles no. A badger gate in a Forestry Commission fence

IN MEMORIAM

strix aluco

1972–1972

It was late one June night. I was driving home along a main road in suburban Buckinghamshire, when I caught sight of a darkish lump in the road, lit up by the sodium lights, about a hundred yards ahead. At this distance it looked like a cardboard box flapping in the traffic's slipstream. Two cars passed over it before me.

When I was within about twenty yards I saw with a shock that it was a large bird, rolled almost flat onto the road, yet with still enough life in it to be thrashing one wing in the air. I stopped and ran over to it, and found the remains of a young tawny owl – fledged that year, to judge by the tufts of down still in its plumage.

It was an appalling wreck of a bird, one wing and most of the body mangled and pulped, the top of its head stoved in. Yet miraculously, it was still alive, fighting – as wild creatures will even through extremes of pain – for the last fragments of its life. From somewhere inside the bloody pile of feathers its hooked beak and down-covered talons tore at me as I bent down towards it. There was no hope of saving it. Yet I couldn't bring myself to wring its neck. I shut my eyes and began to stamp hard on its skull, again and again, until it had stopped shuddering. I found it obscene and shocking to have been part of the ugly process by which this bird was killed. Had it been run down in the dark and privacy of a country lane I might have found my executioner's role a little easier. Here, on a glaring suburban carriageway as clinical and sterile as an operating theatre, it seemed a senseless slaughter: two creatures with no interest in each other whatsoever collide; those eyes that are so exquisitely and efficiently adapted that they can see in one hundred times less light than a human yet are no match for a headlight beam, were dazzled, crushed, and finally stamped into the ground.

I can understand that it is sometimes difficult to avoid a temporarily blinded bird. But I cannot forgive a man who leaves a maimed owl dying in the road. If he had once had to kill a struggling bird in the flesh, I think he might drive a little more compassionately in the future.

I shifted the corpse into the gutter. It was the final insult, but someone might have passed it by and been chastened for a moment.

Smoke and fumes

In a single year, the total pollution produced by British cars amounts to more than 6 million tons of carbon monoxide, 300,000 tons of hydrocarbons, 210,000 tons of oxides of nitrogen, 20,000 tons of sulphur dioxide, 10,000 tons of aldehydes, 7,000 tons of lead, a great deal of smoke, and unquantifiable amounts of solid particles ranging from asbestos brake dust to rubber particles. We know very little yet about the effects these vast quantities of chemicals may be having on human life and it may seem misplaced to worry about the effects on wildlife. Nevertheless, there is evidence of effects in the natural world, and they may rebound back on us in the long run.

The most obvious and direct influence of exhaust fumes is on roadside vegetation. In Brighton, so many flowers have been killed by traffic fumes that the Parks Department is considering ending floral displays near busy roads. In California, most of the eight million dollars' worth of damage done to crops every year because of air pollution has been blamed on motor vehicles.

Just which component of the fumes is most responsible for killing plants and slowing down their growth is uncertain. Unburnt petrol causes necrosis – a kind of drying-out of the surface of leaves. Ethylene, one of the exhaust hydrocarbons, reduces flowering by 50 per cent in high concentrations. Soot and oil can clog up leaves, preventing them transpiring and in extreme cases shutting out the light they need to manufacture food. You can see this last effect most clearly on the vegetation growing along the edges of heavily used roads. The plants that have survived will be coated with a layer of soot, mud and oil as thoroughly and evenly as if it had been spread on by an aerosol spray. Along the centre reservation of the M4, between Heathrow Airport and west London, virtually no vegetation has been able to survive at all.

If there is outright chemical poisoning as well, sulphur dioxide is the most likely culprit. The damage this acidic gas does to sensitive plants like lichens is well-known. Admittedly, lichens are a special case. They are not one plant but two, a simple food-producing alga and a fungus shell living in partnership. Having no roots they must take their nourishment as it comes – from the rainwater trickling down the tree trunk or wall on which they live. And they have little choice but to drink up the contamination in the water as well, a significant part of which is the sulphurous acid formed when sulphur dioxide dissolves in water.

Not the sort of lichen growth you will often find in areas of heavy traffic or industry. Pollution is not the only car-borne force that keeps it down: 'The slipstream of cars tends to blast them off the nearside of trees. In one place they were wiped off above a fence but not below it'. Observation by 16-year-old Crawford Lindsay in the 'ACE/Sunday Times Air Pollution Survey' (1972). There is a full account of this survey and of techniques for estimating air pollution by lichen distribution in The Pollution Handbook.

Plants growing in the ground are better off. By the time the rainwater reaches their roots it may have been partially neutralised by chemicals in the soil. But their tissues are fundamentally no different to those in a lichen, and it is difficult to believe that they are totally immune to sulphur dioxide. In heavily built-up areas where both traffic and power stations are pumping vast quantities of this gas into the air, only a few tough lichen species are able to survive. The lichen distribution map follows the outlines of our urban areas with discomforting accuracy.

If the amount of sulphur dioxide in the air continues to soar at its current rate (there was *three times* as much pumped out by Central Electricity Generating Board stations in 1970 as in 1950) we may find the distribution maps of some of our higher plants beginning to shape up in the same way.

But it may turn out that those 7,000 tons of lead are the most serious hazard of all, to wildlife and humans alike. About two grams of lead in the form of the organic compound lead tetra-ethyl are added to every gallon of petrol as an anti-knock agent, to prevent spontaneous ignition of the fuel when it is compressed in the cylinder. Engines run more smoothly when it's used and fuel consumption is reduced as a result. When the petrol is burnt, small amounts of lead are deposited in the exhaust system and oil filters, but at least 75 per cent is emitted as a fine spray of inorganic lead compounds in the exhaust fumes. These particles may be breathed in by animals close to the road, fall to the ground, coating soil, wild flowers and crops, or be washed into drainage ditches round the field edges.

We know a good deal about the effects of lead on the human body, chiefly because of some unpleasant accidents near factories which work with lead compounds. It has proved one of the most insidiously poisonous of all metals – and not just in large doses. Like arsenic, lead accumulates in the body, and the end result of absorbing small quantities of lead compounds over a period of time is much the same as taking a large single dose. It interferes with just about every process in the body, with the kidneys, nerves, blood and reproductive system. So wide-ranging are its effects that there's little agreement about what a 'safe' dose is; and as usual in cases where big financial interests are at stake, the conventionally accepted figure is as high as the authorities dare make it. Yet there is absolutely no doubt now that even relatively low levels of lead in the blood are connected with brain damage and hyperactivity in children (see *Lancet* no 7783).

So far the most alarming evidence of the effect of exhaust-fume lead on animal life has come, not surprisingly, from the USA. In Staten Island Zoo, New York, in 1971 there was an outbreak of inexplicable disease and death amongst a wide variety of creatures. A young leopard began to lose its fur, stopped eating and died the day after being admitted to the New York Medical College. Three weeks later another leopard was found paralysed in its cage.

Exhaustive tests on this animal showed that he was suffering from severe lead poisoning. A quick check on the remains of the first leopard revealed that he too was riddled with lead. Back at the zoo the animal pathologists working on the case discovered that snakes had been dying after losing muscular co-ordination. A horned owl had lost its feathers. The tissues of these animals – and virtually every other one examined – contained levels of lead well above those generally reckoned to be toxic to man. Significantly, they were highest in those animals living in outdoor enclosures.

The search for the source of the poisoning took in bedding, water, food supplies and the paint on the cages. None of these had a lead content remotely high enough to explain what had happened. The most likely source emerged when it was discovered that the surface soil in the outdoor cages contained 4,000 parts per million of lead compounds (the average amount of lead in natural rock is 1·5ppm) and that the ground foliage and grass were contaminated to levels normally only found on road verges (5–1,000ppm; in uncontaminated vegetation the lead content ranges between 0·4–2·0ppm).

Dr Ralph Strebel of the New York Medical College who directed the survey had no hesitation in pointing the finger of blame: 'We can only conclude that most of the lead taken in by the animals resulted from atmospheric fallout'.

Little experimental work has been done on the ecological effects of exhaust-lead contamination in this country, but a pilot study by Philip Williamson of Durham University in 1971 gives some cause for concern. He made exacting measurements of the quantities of lead present in the soil and in the vegetation, insects and animals living on a number of road verges. His samples were taken from sites at varying distances from the road edges of up to 300 feet – which was well into the adjacent farmland. He not only analysed chemically the amount of lead in soil, plants and animals at these different stations, but also measured their population densities, to see if these showed any connection with the concentrations of lead.

The results were mixed. There were no differences in the populations or distributions of any plants or animals that could not be attributed to changes in soil, drainage and management as you moved from verge to field. Nor was there any evidence of overt poisoning. Yet the levels of lead in soil and living matter alike increased steadily the nearer they were to the road. Levels approaching 200ppm were found in the soil of the central reservation of one dual carriageway (compared with 70ppm in a nearby field). Woodlice on the verges had astonishingly high contents of up to 700ppm. Lead in the spleens and kidneys of verge shrews and mice was four or five times higher than in those from the farmland.

But the most disturbing results concerned the vegetation alongside the Catterick bypass section of the A1. This is a dual carriageway with 75 feet of sloping verge and carrying, according to the County Surveyor, something like 34,000 vehicles a day. The field behind the verge was, that year, under pasture for sheep. These are the results Philip Williamson found for this road: (see overleaf)

These results may seem insignificant beside those formidable levels in the Staten Island Zoo. But remember that although Britain has casually decided that there is no need for any limit to the amount of lead in human foodstuffs, the World Health Organisation recommends a level of 5ppm as being the safe maximum. That field near Catterick, which could well carry wheat in a few years, had more than double this concentration for its whole area.

Car exhausts are not the only sources of potent chemicals on the

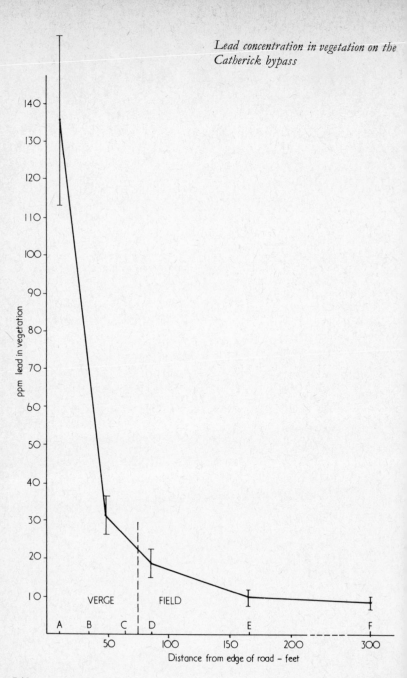

Lead concentration in vegetation on the Catherick bypass

road. In some north country areas that are subject to heavy snow falls, the highway authorities will spray salt onto the motorways at concentrations of up to 14lb per foot length. Over the whole of Britain something like a million and a half tons of salt are spread on the roads every winter. Most of this eventually drains off onto the verges; and though some botanists believe that we may yet see miniature saltmarshes along our iciest trunk roads, at the moment the brine does nothing but harm, and can cause considerable stunting of tree growth.

Off the road

All trackways, from footpaths to motorways, have certain features in common. They're open strips of country, kept stable by the way they are used, and with a built-in carrier service in the shape of whatever travels along them.

Canals and railways fit perfectly into this pattern. The canal system has in effect added thousands of miles of interconnected artificial river to our countryside, as well as the towpaths and hedges that border them. Water plants have colonised the banks and spread throughout the system including some curious aliens, introduced by the commercial traffic or encouraged by the character of the canal itself.

Orange balsam, with its mottled, nasturtium-like flowers, was introduced into this country from America as a garden flower. By the beginning of the nineteenth century it had escaped into the wild and was found growing along the edge of a river in Surrey in 1822. From there it spread rapidly along the banks of our waterways, showing a distinct preference for canals. The reason behind its successful colonisation lies in the seeds. The seed pods of all members of the balsam family have the habit of exploding violently when they're ripe and hurling their fruits several feet away. The fruits of the orange balsam have the extra advantage of being light and corky enough to float on water. So once it had reached our waterway system the plant was in a strong position. Catapulted off into the water, the seeds floated away through the system until they lodged in a bank. Where there was no way through by water, birds, anglers and boatmen no doubt inadvertently helped them on their way. The plant's success along canals may be because the

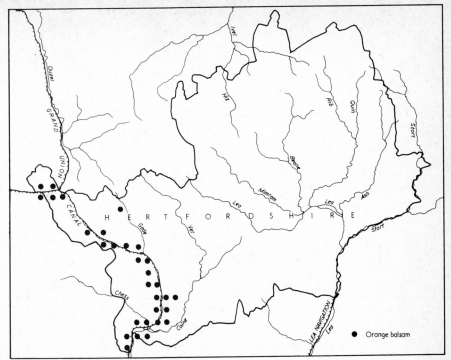

A map of the distribution of orange balsam in Hertfordshire. The way this balsam clings to the canal and yet is absent from most of the natural waterways is very striking.

slowness of the current gives the fruits a better chance of making a beachhead.

To do justice to the wildlife and particularly the flora of the railways would need a book to itself. Any commuter who prefers looking out of the window to poring over his newspaper will be aware that railway embankments have one of the richest and most varied collections of wild flowers of any habitat in our island.

The story behind the success of railside flora is not so different to that of the motorways. Railway embankments and cuttings are well-drained, sunny, undisturbed except by the foolhardy, and suffer no more damage at the hands of their managers, British Rail, than an occasional burn-off or burst of scrub clearance. Hence those marvellously dense colonies of primrose and cowslip and meadow cranesbill can flourish undisturbed in the cuttings as they do in few other environments.

But some of the most fascinating plant stories associated with the railways have the trains, not the embankments, as their heroes. Like cars and Roman sandals, trains are efficient carriers of all sorts of seeds, sometimes ferrying them physically, but more often wafting them along in their slipstream. So you can find Australian and South American weeds, sprung from seeds caught up in imported fleeces and dropped from wool wagons, growing in the goods sidings near mill towns. Flowers more usually associated with seaside shingle like wall-pepper, dark-green mouse-ear, strapwort and scurvy grass have found their way to equally congenial homes amongst the granite ballast at the edge of the tracks. And those who lament the passing of steam may be saddened to learn that this has also meant an end to the migrations of many West Country ferns, whose spores rode the rods east and settled in the damp stonework (which was kept moist by the steam) at the entrance of tunnels and under north-facing platforms.

Wild carrot along the Birmingham to Euston line near Boxmoor

Conclusion:
Coping with the car

I am writing this at the beginning of 1974, as the full implications of the fuel crisis are beginning to become apparent. Travelling on wheels is plainly never going to be the same again. A 50mph speed limit has been imposed. Petrol prices have risen by more than 10p a gallon in two months, and the average number of miles driven per week has fallen by about 10 per cent. It looks encouragingly likely that many of the improvements in the design and social role of automobiles that may have come about eventually because of enlightened self-interest, will now be rushed through because of economic necessity. Cars will become smaller, engines more efficient, and their exhausts less polluting as a result. Our style of travelling is likely to change, and maybe our whole conception of mobility. Leg-power will become more important; roads will lose their dominance over other sorts of trackways. And one day, perhaps, the quality of a journey will be valued as much as its speed and distance. These changes are likely to have as great a long-term effect upon the wildlife of waysides as the introduction of the automobile itself.

But meanwhile we will still drive, park, choke up country lanes, run down owls. New roads will be built – if less frenziedly – and old ones widened. The scaling-down of the supremacy of the private car over the next decade or so is not instantly going to ease the pressures on our embattled and diminishing countryside. Already the car – like other territorially expansive creatures – is transforming the environment to meet its own needs. The

landscape of travel is turning in on itself, becoming self-sufficient. We are well into the era of 'going out for a spin', not to anywhere in particular but just to enjoy the freedom – often illusory – of moving about at will. On motorways you cannot even stop, and the natural landscape has been shaped for the benefit of those travelling at 6omph. The destination becomes not so much a place as another road on which you *can* stop, even if it is unwillingly in a congested beauty-spot lane. At the end of the journey, be it traffic jam or marshalled picnic site, the view is likely to be the same: thousands of creatures of your own kind, shoulder to shoulder on the bare ground. It is the familiar prospect of all population explosions.

So what are the alternatives? One, which seems less impractical in the wake of the fuel crisis, is to abandon the internal combustion engine and maybe the whole system of private transport based upon it. There could be more trains for long journeys, boats, trams, horses, bikes and legs for short. All of them are a good sight safer and healthier for travellers and the environment than the automobile. But by themselves they aren't quite sufficient. They don't really cope with the needs of those who live in isolated areas, or who have to make long out-of-the-way journeys. They penalise the old, the sick and the very young, who may not have the strength to walk or bike long distances; just as, incidentally, the appalling state of public transport penalises these non-car-owning groups at present. And there is still to be considered that obstinate urban refugee – be he tourist or full-blown naturalist – who wakes on a May morning wanting urgently to see the sea-pinks on a Welsh cliff before the weekend is over.

Some sort of personal, motorised vehicle is a vital part of a socially equitable transport system, though as I shall suggest briefly at the end of this chapter, the ideal 'car' would bear little resemblance to the machines we drive today. But if we are to continue with private transport, there must be very much greater control of it in both town and countryside than at present.

Current experiments in countryside traffic control fall into three main categories, which I shall call 'quarantining', 'honeypotting' and 'dispersal'. Quarantining puts certain key areas of country out-of-bounds to vehicles. Honeypotting aims to achieve the same result by positive provision, rather than by exclusion. It provides a small number of well-endowed foci – picnic sites, country parks, etc – which can attract and accommodate large numbers of cars and visitors, and hopefully relieve the pressure on more vulnerable sites. Dispersal aims to minimise the effects of traffic by spreading it thinly over a large area. None of these three approaches is *the* solution. Which one is going to be most useful in a given area depends on how many people visit it, what they come for, how open the landscape is, even on the nature of the local soil. In fact in most regions some sort of combination of the three is likely to be needed. To give some idea of how each one can work out in practice, I've collected some brief case histories below.

Quarantining

Aldeburgh Corporation barricaded the sandy dunes between the coast road and the sea in 1969 by raising an earth rampart along the side of the road. This stretch of sandy grassland running north from the town had become the town's unofficial car park. During the holiday months, as caravans and hot-dog stalls began to join the private cars, it began to resemble a coastal shanty town. The corporation acted before the area was ruined for all visitors. They banned haphazard parking along the whole length of the road except in two official parking areas, and built the bank (from pulverised household refuse and imported soil) to prevent cars driving over the sand.

The results in terms of the look of the place were dramatic. You could begin to see that the area was dune grassland, and not just a sandpit. Within a couple of years native dune flowers, grasses and sedges had started to bind the sand together again; and a very attractive collection they made, the mats of purple sea pea, yellow wall-pepper and white sea campion. As a bonus, there was also a fascinating border of annuals and escaped garden flowers growing along the disturbed soil on the bank. In June 1971, two years after the dunes were put out-of-bounds to vehicles, I counted over 130 species of plant along half a mile of the coast road. The list included such comparatively scarce species of sandy wastes as henbane, bur medick, sand catchfly and scotch thistle, all of which were once much commoner along the Suffolk coast. As a matter of policy the Council decided to allow these flowers to flourish along the verge to provide a sanctuary for threatened local plants.

(opposite) *Henbane, one of the plants of the Aldeburgh verge, see p 150*

Henbane is used today to provide valuable sedative drugs like hyoscine and atropine, but its history in medicine is rather a dark one. Dr Crippen used it as the source of his poisonous potions, and because there is a certain resemblance between henbane's brown seed pods and a row of decrepit molars, the early herbalists used the plant against toothache. The sufferers were no doubt doped out of their misery for a while, but sometimes conned out of their purses at the same time:

> The seed is used by Mountibank tooth-drawers which run about the country, to cause worms to come forth of the teeth, by burning it in a chafing dish of coles, the party holding his mouth over the fume thereof: but some crafty companions to gain money convey small lute-strings into the water, persuading the patient, that those small creepers came out of his mouth or other parts which he intended to ease.
>
> from Gerard's *The Herball* (1597)

This was a basic and somewhat fortuitous exercise in quarantining. Most experiments make rather more positive provisions for displaced motorists. Probably the most famous of all was that run in the Goyt Valley in Derbyshire in the summer of 1970.

The Goyt Valley is in the Peak District National Park, an area which, because of its great variety of landscape and recreational facilities, can attract over 100,000 cars on a fine Sunday in summer. The results are the familiar ones we have seen throughout this book: congested country lanes, eroded footpaths, litter, fires, compacted soil around tree roots. As a Peak Park Planning Board cartoon had it: 'A view *from* an unscreened car park . . . might be lovely, but a view of it could be terrible . . .'

The Park Planning Board decided to mount an experiment in the valley to provide an escape from the constrictions of the private car. A number of car parks were opened on the perimeter of the area and a minibus laid on to take visitors to picnic sites and rambling

Downland car parking area. Uncontrolled, on the road

Controlled, on the chalk

routes. The experiment was a huge success, particularly during fine weather when it freed the roads of dangerous traffic and the view of a mass of parked cars, whilst only very slightly reducing the individual's freedom to move about as he pleased.

The AA ran a similar experiment at a number of beauty spots on a Sunday afternoon in 1972. As in the Goyt Valley, motorists found they had an alternative to adding their cars to the view: free car parking facilities off the road, and a free minibus service to the beauty spot itself. At the Stack Rocks, on the Pembrokeshire coast, where motorists had no choice but to take the minibus, 85 per cent felt that their day had either been improved or at least not diminished in enjoyment by the scheme. On the White Horse Hills, where there was a choice, 36 per cent agreed to participate in the minibus service, 51 per cent insisted on their right to drive to the summit, and 13 per cent turned away. Taking all the sites in the experiment into account, less than 9 per cent felt that the schemes had spoilt their enjoyment in any way. Most of these gave very practical reasons for their reluctance to leave their cars – they wanted shelter, personal cooking facilities, or had young, elderly or infirm passengers to carry.

Honeypotting

All schemes of this sort that encourage cars to park in prescribed areas are practising a kind of honeypotting as well as quarantining. The aim of honeypotting is to ensure that one particular area of a region is so attractive that the public is drawn to it, and away from more vulnerable regions.

With scenic drives, the road itself is made the honeypot. A route is chosen along a network of roads which are hopefully able to take extra traffic, and which pass through attractive and representative scenery. A typical drive is the 70-mile circular trail laid by the Scottish Wildlife Trust between Perth, Dunkeld, Aberfeldy and Gilmerton. The Trust produced a booklet for those following the trail which explained how the landscape had been formed, and pointed out points of interest, picnic sites, etc.

The danger of scenic drives is that they must, by definition, concentrate traffic into scenically attractive countryside which all too often means small villages and narrow lanes. But it is comparatively easy to avoid these harmful effects by a careful choice of route.

A much greater danger is raised when *new* roads are proposed to give the public greater access to large areas of open country. The arguments in favour of such roadbuilding can be very persuasive: traffic is drained from secondary roads, village streets and country lanes, and less people are tempted to flock to lonely and unspoilt corners. But curiously, this line of argument does not square up with the support given to the 'improvement' of the A66 through the Lake District. There, the inspector conducting the public enquiry wrote that the changes to the road would 'reveal new views of the surroundings to those who travel on the roads and so increase their enjoyment'. It would be selfish to find fault with such sentiments. Yet it is undeniably true that where new views are opened up, so fresh visitors will be tempted in – most likely still inside their cars. And where there are new roads there will be new hotels, new filling stations and maybe even new towns.

There is an absolute argument against the literal application of this 'window on the wild' philosophy when wildernesses like Dartmoor are concerned. The character and value of such areas is completely negated unless their remoteness is preserved. But can this be done whilst still preserving the public's right of access?

One solution is to grade the roads inside National Parks and wilderness areas much more exactly in terms of the landscape they pass through and the traffic they can cope with. The chief arterial routes are best sited round the perimeter of the area. They should be well provided with parking spaces and, if possible, with minibus services into 'the interior'. Existing roads through the area, if they are kept open, should be restricted in size and weight of vehicles which can use them. Some lanes to the more remote areas might be toll-gated, and closed after a given number of cars had entered – this system has worked very well in the USA. In large regions of open country, like the Scottish Highlands, there might be room to allow very rough roads to remain open, with their boulders and craters intact. But everywhere there ought to be part of the heartland which is kept completely free of vehicles and man-made artefacts.

The key is a variety of roads, tailored to the needs of both landscape and visitors.

Dispersal

With a variety of roads we are really into the area of dispersal – the 'spreading thin' approach. This usually works best in large areas, where comparatively high numbers of visitors can be incorporated into the landscape, or where there is abundant woodland cover to disguise car parks. The New Forest has 200 sites where day visitors can drive off the public roads and enter the Forest. In Ashridge Park, in Hertfordshire, the National Trust has provided dozens of roadside parking places amongst the trees. Each one is between one and five acres in extent and is barricaded off from the surrounding woodland by ditches and rows of stakes. This is normally a sufficient area not only to accommodate the cars, but to provide space for picnicking and ball games.

In all such sites 'losing' the cars by landscaping the area amongst the trees is crucial. The Department of the Environment is currently experimenting with the same principle along some trunk roads and motorways, where it is developing roadside picnic areas. One near Brandon Creek in Cambridgeshire covers $2\frac{1}{2}$ acres, has been extensively planted with mature trees, and is provided with tables, benches and litter bins.

The same county has produced one of the nicest examples of how the interests of tourists and naturalists can be reconciled. Cherry Hinton chalk pits, inside the city boundaries of Cambridge, are well known for their ancient wild cherry trees and the rare perfoliate honeysuckle. In 1970 the pits were leased to the Caravan Club. This could have spelled the destruction of this small but fascinating habitat, but for a model exercise in collaboration between the Club and the Cambridge Naturalists' Trust. The two organisations agreed to restrict access to the pits to their respective members, and to produce a booklet about the site, which would be available to all visitors from a warden. They also opened a record book in the warden's office in which they invited all visitors to record any interesting observations. If anything, Cherry Hinton pits have improved as a habitat since this arrangement, and it is impossible to escape the lesson – that it is far more productive in the long term to invite participation than to fence out.

But however much cars are managed in the countryside, they are, at present, a menace to all living things. An ecologically acceptable vehicle would not just be a 'safety' car but an 'organic' one, fitting in as far as possible with the needs of *all* the creatures it has to share space with. Space is a key notion; the ecological car would occupy less than a third of the road space of the modern saloon – 9,000 square inches has been recommended as the maximum. It would be powered by electricity, or some other non-polluting energy source, and would be restricted in its power (and therefore energy consumption), its top speed, and the amount of noise it could make.

Ideally it would be automated on trunk roads and only be put back into a human's unsteady hands when it was on a side road and unlikely to meet much other traffic.

It is surely not beyond the wit of our car manufacturers – always paraded as the spearhead of British technology – to mass-produce a car of this sort. It is inevitable that they will have to sooner or later, and it seems criminal to wait until yet more of our towns and countryside are defiled. If not, at least we have our bikes, in energy terms the most efficient form of travelling on land ever devised – more efficient in fact than any animal, let alone man-made machine.

It would be wrong to become snobbishly hostile to the car. Many people are not able to walk or bike long distances. More are uncomfortable about venturing into wild countryside away from the secure combination of lounge, picnic-hamper, carrycot and backpack that the family car has become. But as I hope I have shown, leaving your car is not only better for the land. It also gives you a chance to meet the natural world face to face.

The motorist and country-law

The wildlife of roadsides is of course covered by such statutes as the Protection of Birds Acts and Cruelty to Animals Acts. But there is in addition a certain amount of legislation which applies specifically to roadsides and verges.

a)   Most road verges are public land and you are entitled to have access to them and to park your car on them. But, except where there are special parking facilities, it is illegal to drive your car more than fifteen yards off a public road. This is true even on common land.

b)   In most counties in Great Britain it is illegal to dig up wild plants from the road verge, and if the Wild Flowers Protection Bill is finally made law it will also be illegal to offer for sale any flowers you have picked. This bill also gives complete protection – prohibiting both uprooting and picking – to some 20 rare species.

c)   It is not illegal, however, to gather 'natural produce' like mushrooms, nuts and berries from wayside hedges and verges. In law such produce has no owner, unlike deliberately cultivated crops.

d)   There is no right to privacy under British law. You may therefore take photographs from the road verge, of views, farmland, hedgerow trees, even private country houses!

Further reading

A A Book of the Countryside (Drive Publications, 1973). Many general notes on roadside flowers, hedges, etc

Aird, Alisdair. *The Automotive Nightmare* (Hutchinson, 1972). The crisis of the car: noise, pollution, congestion

Bonser, K. J. *The Drovers* (Macmillan, 1970)

Brooks, Paul. *Roadless Areas* (Sierra Club/Ballantin, 1971). Includes a chapter on roadless wilderness areas in the US

Buckle, E. M. 'Report on an Enquiry into the Measures Taken to Conserve Wild Flora on Grass Verges by Various County Authorities in the UK 1970–71' (Settle and District Civic Society, 1971)

Bulfield, Anthony. *The Icknield Way* (Terence Dalton, 1972)

Christian, Garth. *Tomorrow's Countryside* (John Murray, 1966). Includes road verges and railways; a most intelligent survey of conservation problems

Coggin, P. A. (ed). *The Birth of a Road* (Hart-Davis, 1974). The account of the Wiltshire Schools M4 project

Council for the Preservation of Rural England. *Loss of Cover through Removal of Hedges and Trees* (1971)

——. *Roads and the Landscape* (1970)

Countryside Commission. *The Weekend Motorist in the Lake District* (HMSO, 1969)

——. *Picnic Sites* (HMSO, 1969)

Crowe, Sylvia. *The Landscape of Roads* (Architectural Press, 1960)

Dennis, Eve (ed). *Everyman's Nature Reserve: Ideas for Action* (David & Charles, 1972)

Dunball, A. P. 'The Management and Planting of Motorway Verges', *The Flora of a Changing Britain*, Botanical Society of the British Isles Report (Pendragon Press, 1970)

Ellis, E. A. *Wild Flowers of the Hedgerow* (Jarrolds, 1973)

Fairbrother, Nan. *New Lives, New Landscapes* (Architectural Press, 1970; Penguin, 1972). Includes a brilliant and imaginative study of the road as habitat and landscape

Forestry Commission. *Conservation of the New Forest* (HMSO, 1970)

——. *Public Recreation in National Forests: A Factual Study* (HMSO, 1967)

Gilmour, John and Walters, Max. *Wild Flowers* (Collins, 1954). Especially Chapter 12 on fields and roadsides

HMSO. *Marshall Committee Report on Highway Maintenance* (1970)

Hoskins, W. G. *The Making of the English Landscape* (Hodder & Stoughton, 1955; Penguin, 1970)

Illich, Ivan. *Energy and Equity* (Calder & Boyers, 1973). Compares the car with less wasteful and more efficient forms of transport – especially the bicycle

Leutscher, A. *The Pond* (Franklin Watts, 1972)

Lousley, J. E. 'The Influence of Transport on a Changing Flora', *The Flora of a Changing Britain*, Botanical Society of the British Isles Report (Pendragon Press, 1970)

Mabey, Richard. *The Unofficial Countryside* (Collins, 1973). On the natural history of urban areas

Mabey, Richard and The Advisory Centre for Education. *The Pollution Handbook* (Penguin Education, 1974). Principally concerned with telling you how to measure pollution yourself.

Mellanby, Kenneth. *Pesticides and Pollution* (Collins, 1967)

Millman, Roger. *Outdoor Recreation in the Highland Countryside* (1971). Published by the author and obtainable from him at the Department of Land Economy, Cambridge

Patmore, J. Allan. *Land and Leisure* (David & Charles, 1970; Penguin, 1972). Includes a very comprehensive study of the leisure motorist in the countryside

Peak Park Planning Board. *What Future for the Peak National Park?* (1972)

Ramblers' Association. *Motor Vehicles in National Parks* (1963)

Salisbury, Sir Edward. *Weeds and Aliens* (Collins, 1961)

Sillitoe, K. K. *Planning for Leisure* (HMSO, 1969)

Way, J. M. *Road Verges on Rural Roads* (Monks Wood Experimental Station – Nature Conservancy, 1973)

—— (ed). *Road Verges: Their Function and Management* (A symposium. Monks Wood Experimental Station – Nature Conservancy, 1969)

—— (ed). *Road Verges in Scotland: Their Function and Management* (A symposium. Nature Conservancy, 1970)

Wheeler, K. S. 'Roadside Verges As an Approach to Environmental Education' (1972). Obtainable from the Geography Department of Leicester College of Education

Williams-Ellis, Clough. *Roads in the Landscape* (HMSO, 1967)

Max Hooper is preparing a volume on hedges for the Collins 'New Naturalist' series. For the same series, J. M. Way is preparing a volume on waysides which will doubtless become the standard scientific work on the subject.

ORGANISATIONS

Environmental Education Resource Project: Roadside Verges. Further information from John Paull, Environmental Studies Adviser, County Hall, Glenfield, Leicester LE3 8RF.

Companions of Save Our Wild Flowers. A newly-formed pressure group with a particular interest in roadside verges. Information from Lady Alice Morland, The High Hall, Thornton-le-Dale, Yorkshire.

Acknowledgements

I should like to thank H. F. Ellis and *The Countryman* magazine for permission to reprint an extract from 'Ornithological Saloons'.

Many people gave advice and information for different sections of this book. I would like to thank especially Dr J. M. Way, of the Monks Wood Experimental Station of the Nature Conservancy; Dr E. M. Buckle of the Settle Civic Society; Colin Ward, Education Officer of the Town and Country Planning Association; Keith Wheeler of the Geography Department, City of Leicester College of Education; Colonel Rooke of the Forestry Commission; G. E. Betts and E. L. Williams, County Surveyors of East and West Suffolk respectively, and David Overton, County Planning Officer for Hertfordshire; D. J. Owen, Town Clerk of Aldeburgh Corporation; the Earl of Cranbrook, President of the Suffolk Naturalists' Society (and many members of that Society and the Norfolk Naturalists' Trust); the organisers of the North-East London Polytechnic's 1973 Symposium on 'Motorways and the Biologist'; and most of all the late Nan Fairbrother, whose inspiration, unfailingly imaginative optimism and vivid writing were the greatest single influence on this book.

If I owe a great debt to her book *New Lives, New Landscapes*, I am also grateful to three authors who very generously allowed me to see manuscript or limited editions of their work: Phillip Williamson for his MSc thesis on the effects of car exhaust lead pollution on roadside ecosystems; P. A. Coggin, director of the Wiltshire Schools M4 project, for a draft of the results of that project; and Dr R. N. Millman for his study 'Outdoor Recreation in the Highland Countryside'.

Acknowledgment for the illustrations is given in the list of illustrations (pp 7–8), but for help far beyond the call of duty I should like to thank Joyce Tuhill and Alastair Robertson who produced, at very short notice and to exceedingly amateur briefs, magnificent line illustrations; Howard Rosen of the publications branch of the Department of the Environment; the Bruce Coleman agency and John and Su Gooders of Ardea Photographics; and Francesca Greenoak, who gave much sensitive advice on the choice of photographs – as did Christine Vincent, whose expertise and sheer hard work in guiding the choice and processing of the photographs was irreplaceable.

There was much miscellaneous help, too. Miranda Cummins did a good deal of the research in tracking down illustrations and references, and Judy Roberts and Diana Harry typed the final manuscript.

Index

broom, 98; in hedges, 57
broomrape, clove-scented, 34
Buckle, Dr E. M., 49
bugloss, viper's, 52
Bulford Camp, 92
bullaces, 67
bullfinch, 116
bumble-bees, verge species, 34, 58
bunting: corn, 82; reed, 71
bustard, Hougara, 115
buttercup, 32, 34, 107
butterflies, 93; green-veined white, 58; orange-tip, 58; verge species, 34
buzzards, 80, 117

caddis fly larva, 74
campions, 34, 57
canal system, 142
car parks, 122, 154
carrot, wild, 144
cars: advantages of, 90; 'ecological', 155; figures on use and ownership, 121–2; as hides, 90, 114–20; and style of travelling, 145
catchfly: Breckland or Spanish, 35, 52; night-scented, 92; sand, 148
Catterick bypass; pollution on, 139
celandine, 21, 32, 33, 58; greater, 21
chaffinch, 58, 115
chalk banks, 93
Cherry Hill, 52
Cherry Hinton chalk pits, 154

cherry trees, in hedges, 57
cigarettes, as fertiliser, 125
Clarke, John, 104
clary, 36
clovers, 24, 38
cobbles, 23
columbine: wild, 104; cultivated, 107
Coprinus atramentarius, 30
coriander, 102
corn bunting, 82
corn-cockle, 21
Cornwall, verge nature reserves, 50
couchgrass, 42
cow parsley, 32, 33, 107
cowslip, 33, 46, 144
cow-wheat, field, 34
crab apple, 65; flowers, 63
cranesbill, meadow, 144
crocuses, naturalised, 37
crows, 80
creeping jenny, 102

daffodils, wild, 98
daisies, 125, ox-eye, 107
dame's violet, 36
damsons, 67
Dartmoor, 153
deer: accidents involving, 126–7; at night, 119; warning notices and mirrors, 127
Defoe, Daniel, 20, 21
Department of the Environment, 98, 154
Derbyshire, verge management schemes, 49

Devon, verge cutting, 49
dispersal, of vehicles, 147, 154
ditches, 19, 26; boundary, 38; dipping in, 72; ditching 41, 70; flowers, 71; maintenance, 70: wild life, 71
diving beetle, great, 76
DNOC weedkiller, 42
dock: curled, 107; broad-leaved, 107
dogwood, 57, 63
Dorset, verge management schemes, 49
dragonfly larva, 74
drains, piped, 70
drove roads, 23, 24
drovers, 23
Druid plant-lore, 36
dual carriageway, central reservations, 108
ducks, in flight, 116
dunnocks, 58
dytiscus larva, 73

East Suffolk County Council, 39, 48
East Suffolk heaths, 122
eels, 71
elder, ground, 68
elderberries, 66
elder flowers, 63
elecampane, 36
Ellis, H. F., 116
elm: Cornish, 57; English, 57; in hedges, 57; small-leaved, 57; wych, 57
embankments, 20, 21, 25

Enclosure, Parliamentary, 20, 54
enclosure roads, 25, 41
erosion, 124
eryngium campestre, 35
exhaust fumes, effects of, 135

fat hen, 94
fennel, 21
ferns, on railways, 144
figwort, water, 72
fire, 122
flail-mower, 45, 55, 56, 61
flax: perennial, 34, 35; purging, 102
fleabane, 72
fleas, water, 73
flixweed, 52
footpaths, 34
Forest of Dean, 127
Forestry Commission, 122, 133
Fosse Way, 20
fox, 119, 120
frogs, 71
fuchsia hedges, 57
furze, 122

gardens, herb and physic, 36, 68
Gerard, John, 68, 150
gibbets, 79, 80
gooseberries, wild, 65
gorse, as hedge, 57
goutweed, 68
Goyt Valley, 17, 150
grain, spilled, 27, 29
grass, cutting, 41

whitethroats, 58, 116
wilderness areas, 153
Wild Flowers Protection Bill, 157
Williams-Ellis, Clough, 21
Williamson, Philip, 139
willow herb: great, 71; rose-bay, 122
Wiltshire, verge management, 45
Wolves Wood, 39
Women's Institutes, 52
woodland flora, 34
woodpeckers, 58, 114; green, 79
worms, 29; earth, 109; mud, 29
woundwort, field, 21

wrens, 58
wych elm, 57

yellowhammers, 58, 116
yellow iris, 71
yellow vetchling, 102
yew, 57
Young Ornithologists' Club, kestrel survey, 109

zoning system for mowing, 46